The Lightning Play

Charlotte Jones' first play, *Airswimming*, was premiered at the Battersea Arts Centre, London, and later broadcast on Radio 4. *In Flame* was premiered in January 1999 at the Bush Theatre, London, and revived at the New Ambassadors, London, in September 2000. *Martha, Josie and the Chinese Elvis* was premiered at the Bolton Octagon in April 1999 and transferred to the Liverpool Everyman in May of that year. It won the *Manchester Evening News* Best Play Award of 1999. Charlotte Jones won the Critics' Circle Award for Most Promising Playwright in 2000 for *In Flame* and *Martha, Josie and the Chinese Elvis. Humble Boy*, was awarded the Susan Smith Blackburn Award 2001, the Critics' Circle Best New Play Award, 2002, and the People's Choice Best New Play Award, 2002. It opened at the Cottesloe Theatre in August 2001 before transferring to the West End, where it ran for nine months. It has since enjoyed productions all over the world. *The Dark* premiered at the Donmar Warehouse in 2003, and in 2004 she wrote the book for the musical of *The Woman in White* (music by Andrew Lloyd Webber, lyrics by David Zippel) which ran in the West End and on Broadway.

CHARLOTTE JONES

The Lightning Play

faber and faber

First published in 2006
by Faber and Faber Limited
3 Queen Square, London WC1N 3AU

Typeset by Country Setting, Kingsdown, Kent CT14 8ES
Printed in England by Bookmarque, Croydon, Surrey

A CIP record for this book
is available from the British Library

ISBN 978–0–571–23374–8
0–571–23374–0

2 4 6 8 10 9 7 5 3 1

For my children

The **Lightning Play** was first performed at the Almeida Theatre, London, on 9 November 2006. The cast , in order of appearance, was as follows:

Max Villiers Matthew Marsh
Eddie Fox Lloyd Hutchinson
Harriet Villiers Eleanor David
Jacklyn Pettit Adie Allen
Imogen Cumberbatch Katherine Parkinson
Burak Simon Kassianides
Marcus Cumberbatch Orlando Seale
Tabby Morris Christina Cole

Director Anna Mackmin
Designer Lez Brotherston
Lighting Designer Tim Mitchell
Sound Designer Paul Groothuis
Cinematography and Projection Designer Jon Driscoll

The text that follows went to press while rehearsals were still in progress, and may therefore differ in some respects from the play as performed.

Characters

Max Villiers

Harriet Villiers

Eddie Fox

Jacklyn Pettit

Imogen Cumberbatch

Marcus Cumberbatch

Tabby Morris

Burak

THE LIGHTNING PLAY

Act One

Halloween. The present day. The set represents Max and Harriet Villiers' front room, and also various other locations both exterior and interior throughout the play. The front room is that of an affluent, North London middle-class couple with exquisite taste. There should be a hint of woodland in the set. Inserted into the back wall, upstage centre perhaps, there is a large black screen which will represent Max and Harriet's new plasma screen TV. In another part of the back wall is a concealed stereo unit and a concealed video/DVD. There should be a wooden ledge with five remote controls on it. There is some furniture – perhaps a large, old, beautifully distressed leather sofa and a few other seats that could resemble tree stumps more than chairs. On the floor, set prominently, there is a large and beautiful kilim-type rug in rich colours. There are perhaps three exits – one as if to the kitchen, one that leads upstairs and one to the hallway leading to the front door.

Music: Sam Cooke, 'Let the Good Times Roll'.

As the house lights fade, the screen flickers into life. All the film, until the very last scene of the play should have a strange, black-and-white home-movie quality to it. We see a wood – as if someone holding a camcorder were running in panic through it. It is a woodland in rain and in murky light. A stormy sky that threatens thunder. The music starts to warp slightly.

The screen fades to black at the same time as the lights fade up on the room. It is about 3 p.m., still daylight.

Max Villiers enters. He is a handsome, fit but fleshy man in his late forties, early fifties; his hair is greying at the sides. He is well dressed in a casual way. He stops a moment and registers the rug on the floor. His brows wrinkle but he moves swiftly to the ledge and looks at the remote controls. He chooses one and moves confidently downstage. He looks at the remote control, selects a button and presses it. The screen remains resolutely blank. He tries again. Then he returns to the ledge and picks up another remote control. He tries again without success. The music fades.

Max (*under his breath*) Oh for fu— Harriet! Harriet!?

When his wife does not answer, he picks up the third remote control. He tries again. Sighs and noises of frustration from Max.

Three thousand pounds' worth of horseshit.

He starts pressing wildly.

(*With angry resignation.*) Well, it's fucked.

The doorbell goes.

Not today, thank you.

He returns to the ledge, takes another remote control, perhaps one he's tried before.

Witness the noble savage, totally in control of his environment. Man and machine, working perfectly together . . .

He tries again. The doorbell goes again.

The screen flickers momentarily into life. We see a picture for a moment, just for a second – a large, ancient yew tree – and then the screen fades to black again.

(*Frantic.*) Ah! Yes! What did I do? What did I do?

4

He presses the remote control frantically. The screen switches to black.

You little bastard. You devious little bastard.

As he says this, Eddie Fox enters. Max does not at first register him. Eddie is the same age as Max but looks older. He's small but genial-looking, a man with tendencies to be a slob. He wears an old unfashionable parka and he carries a plastic bag – it contains an egg sandwich, a bottle of water, four cans of beer and perhaps something from the hardware shop. He looks at Max and works out what he's trying to do. He walks up to him, looking at the screen. They stand together a moment. Without looking at him, Max at last speaks to him.

(*Still concentrated on the screen.*) Eddie.

Eddie I used the key you lent me.

Max (*absorbed by the screen*) Excellent.

Eddie You got the new telly, then.

Max Can't get the bastard to work. I am condemned to this looking-through-a-glass-darkly hell-type experience.

Eddie Do you want me to have a go?

Max (*ignoring this offer*) Three thousand pounds. Top of the range. The zenith of plasma screens. Its resolution is second to none; the surround sound caresses your eardrums; its pixels are pitched to perfection; it whispers sweet nothings to you as you gently fall asleep in front of its flickering light. I've got it all here – seventy-one inches of perfection. I am a man in technology heaven. Only problem – can't switch the fucker on.

Eddie Is there an instruction booklet?

Max I've paid three thousand pounds for this – I haven't got time to read instructions. It should respond to my

5

voice, it should know my touch; it should be down on all fours tugging at my zip.

Eddie It's very nice.

Max The black is deeper than on any other plasma TV.

Eddie It looks good. When did you get it?

Max They installed it this morning. I should have been here. I had to meet Tabitha Morris.

Eddie (*with a smile*) Oh yes! It was today. Of course.

Max Yes . . . Why does it need four remote controls? What earthly good is that?

Eddie It's for the various inputs, isn't it? Terrestrial, Sky, DVD . . . perhaps.

Max looks at him suspiciously.

Max (*still trying with the various remote controls*) It came on for a minute. I had it. Then I lost it again. I don't think they've tuned it in properly.

Eddie (*with a chuckle*) Think I'll stick to my portable black-and-white.

Eddie rummages in his plastic bag and gets out a four-pack of beer.

Drink?

Max Bloody good idea . . . Sorry. Heard you ring. Thought you were one of the disaffected youth of today.

Eddie What?

Max Trick or treat. What an asbo-abomination that is.

Eddie (*looking at his watch*) Bit early, isn't it?

Max They don't give a shit these days. They start Halloween in the middle of August.

Eddie hands him a can.

A treat, thank you.

Eddie So how was Miss Morris? Did she like you? Is it going to work?

Max The researcher's job is yours.

Max sits. Eddie follows suit.

Eddie Really?

Max I am almost certainly going to be the official unofficial autobiographer of Tabby Morris, glamour model and businesswoman *extraordinaire*. The girl with the golden orbs.

Eddie That's fantastic, Max. Well done. Is she nice?

Max She took me by surprise. I felt like I knew her.

Pause.

Eddie A good subject, then?

Max Oh yes. Perfect. She's a walnut whip of contradictions.

Eddie Where did you meet?

Max That new restaurant on the High Street. All very Eurotrash. I was horribly early. She was fashionably late.

Eddie greatly enjoys the following, not in a lewd way, but as Max's audience.

Her breasts arrived separately of course. They had their own chauffeur. She is remarkably pretty – beautiful face – but the whole eyeline thing is very tricky. Her bosom is difficult to avoid.

Eddie How big is it?

Max Oh, it's a big bosom. Big-as-a-baby big. Each one.

Eddie (*a bit worried*) Gosh.

Max Of course I can see she expects me to make a pass at her. Drool a little. That perhaps this book cannot even be written unless I undertake to fondle the breasts. Give each its due weight. Thing is, I fear her breasts, Eddie. I've never been a breast aficionado and these go beyond breasts. My penis is literally shrivelling in fear. But Tabby Morris needs to be needed. So I tell her I'd googled her that morning and that seemed to perk her up. Over 400,000 entries and she's only twenty-five. Same age as Anna.

Eddie And I'd never even heard of her.

Max We are of course talking about two volumes to her story. Before and after the breasts. Did it all to spite her father. Got her first million by the time she was twenty-two. Oh there's meat there, let me tell you, real meat.

Eddie You liked her though?

Max Well, in my game, it doesn't really matter. I must step into her extraordinarily high shoes, I must walk her walk, find her voice. My prose must be girly and breathless and very very 'estuary'.

Eddie Blimey.

Max (*apeing the voice*) 'I had no sense of self until I met my surgeon. Within a week I was having intimate relations with a Formula One star.'

Eddie I feel a bit sorry for her.

Max No need. She's got her head firmly screwed on. Which is a good job. She has a trick to balance as it is. I may offer her a rucksack at our next encounter.

Eddie You're cruel.

Max Best to get it all out now.

Pause.

What would the monks say, eh?

Eddie smiles.

Best thing is, she's given me her home videos.

Eddie What sort of home videos?

Max (*interrupting him*) I DON'T KNOW! But that is
why it is imperative to get this home entertainment
system up and running. I'll go and get them.

*Max exits with a skip. Eddie sits in his parka and sips
from his can, looking at the plasma screen. He stands
up and wanders to the ledge to look at the remote
controls. He picks one up. As he does so, Harriet
Villiers enters. She is Max's wife, slightly younger than
Max and a beautiful woman. She is pale and delicate,
almost ghostly-looking. She enters in a strange,
purposeful way. Such is the strangeness of her entrance
that Eddie goes to speak and then doesn't. He watches
her. She does not see him. She walks over to the rug.
She takes a deep breath. She removes her shoes. Slowly
she kneels on the rug. Then, as if she were doing yoga,
she stretches herself out on it and lies prostrate on it. It
is a sensual move: she breathes slowly, almost as if she
is inhaling the scent of the rug. Eddie watches a
moment, both enthralled and embarrassed. Finally he
speaks.*

Eddie Umm.

Harriet (*face down in the rug, startled*) Oh God.

Eddie Harriet?

Harriet sits herself up swiftly, looks at Eddie.

Harriet Oh dear God. What are you trying to do to me –?

9

Eddie I think Mecca's the other way.

Harriet What?

Eddie Mecca. If you were after Mecca . . .

Harriet Why would I be after Mecca?

Eddie No reason. No reason at all.

Harriet Don't look at me.

Eddie I'm not.

Harriet You were watching me.

Eddie I was merely looking in your direction –

Harriet I was having a . . . personal moment –

Eddie Excellent. As it should be.

Harriet You have this terrible propensity to always be there.

Eddie I'm going to see someone about it. Truly.

Harriet (*pained*) Eddie Fox. When will I be rid of you?

Eddie Imminently. Just say the word.

Harriet I think I will be all right, I will be able to cope when I am finally rid of you.

Eddie Absolutely. I'm sorry, Harriet. I didn't see anything – I wasn't really looking . . .

Harriet has snapped back to normal and is up, straightening out the rug.

Harriet What? What! I was just – trying it out. It's new. I needed to try it out. To see. That's all.

Max re-enters holding some videos and DVDs.

Max What's new?

Eddie The rug. Harriet was trying it out – for size.

Max (*to his wife*) Let me guess – you bought it in the sale.

Harriet I didn't buy it.

Max You stole it? At last Harriet shows some consumer enterprise.

Harriet You really are insufferable. I have the rug on loan. I am seeing whether I can live in harmony with it.

Max Oh Christ. It's a rug, not a world religion.

Harriet It's an East Anatolian prayer mat, actually. It's a semi-antique.

Max A *semi*-antique?! They saw you coming, darling.

Harriet This rug was woven with care and love and it has withstood sixty years of prayer and struggle and bloodshed. It is a precious thing. It needs to be treated with reverence.

Eddie It's beautiful. The colours.

Harriet Oh shut up. (*To Max.*) It took me a long time to choose it. You hadn't even noticed it.

Max I cannot be expected to keep track of every new object of beauty you bring into the house. I am not the fucking curator.

Harriet I needed the rug to balance out that huge monstrosity on the wall.

Eddie He can't switch it on.

Max Traitor.

Harriet laughs.

Harriet Oh dear.

She looks at the videos.

What a shame. Can't waste your afternoon watching films and drinking beer?

Max Will you do it for me? Darling? Please?

Harriet What do you think?

Eddie It's research.

Max (*a warning, this is a sore subject*) Eddie.

Eddie Tabitha Morris research. I'm helping him.

Harriet Lovely, a bit of light porn in the early afternoon. I thought there was a funny smell in here. You know, darling, you're a bit too old for a mid-life crisis.

Max I'm a late developer.

Harriet Just make sure you keep it off my rug. I might have to take it back.

She goes to go.

Max (*knowing this is not going to go down well*) Oh yes. Before I forget. Some people coming round. Tonight.

Harriet What?

Max Some people. Tonight.

Harriet What people?

Max Just for drinks.

Harriet What people, Max?

Max Imogen and Marcus Cumberbatch.

Harriet Who on earth are they?

Max Imogen. Anna's Imogen. From school.

Harriet Imogen Randall? The plain girl?

Max Hockey thighs.

Harriet What possessed you?

Max I bumped into her. Out of the blue. She's very pregnant.

Harriet All the more reason for her to stay at home, surely?

Max It was a spur-of-the-minute thing.

Harriet You never want people round.

Eddie I'm round all the time.

Harriet I know.

Max Eddie is not people. Eddie is Eddie.

Harriet I may as well not be here.

Max Harriet, I can't do it by myself. She's so pregnant, they won't stay long.

Harriet tuts and goes to go.

Harriet I'm not making any preparations. I'm not up to it. Not today.

Max Good. Excellent. It's a lovely rug.

Harriet You're pathetic.

She exits.

Max (*to Eddie, distracted – his mood has plummeted*) You'll come too, yes?

Eddie I don't know if Harriet –

Max She's fine. You know what she's like. She loves entertaining. Lives for it.

Eddie Can I bring someone?

Max What someone?

Eddie Someone I met today.

Max A woman someone?

Eddie Yes. A woman.

Max You is sly, Mr Fox. Where did you meet her?

Eddie Um. On the Heath.

Max Romantic. So you asked her out? Just like that.

Eddie Yes. Yes.

Max Today?

Eddie Yes.

Max A complete stranger?

Eddie Well –

Max And she said yes?

Eddie Yes.

Max About bloody time.

Eddie So I can bring her?

Max Of course you can bring her. That's made my day, Eddie. I can't tell you – here – shake my hand.

Eddie smiles wanly.

I'd better just check on Harriet. You'll be –

Eddie Yes, yes, mate, fine go ahead.

Max exits

There is a sudden lighting change on stage. Eddie pulls his parka around him.

SCENE TWO

Exterior, Hampstead Heath. The same day, but earlier in the morning. It is drizzly. Eddie sits, takes out an egg sandwich from his plastic bag. Jacklyn Pettit enters – she is in her late thirties, hippyish, not unattractive, dressed in rambler's attire. She smiles at Eddie as she approaches him. She has perhaps a faint West Country burr to her voice.

Jacklyn Here comes trouble!

Eddie What?

Jacklyn Having your lunch?

Eddie Yes.

Jacklyn Do you mind if I –?

Eddie No, no!

She sits down next to him.

Sorry, it's egg.

Jacklyn Have you got another one? I'm starving.

He gives her a sandwich.

It's rambling does it to me – gives me an appetite. I love it, though – I mean normally wilder than this – you know, Hampstead Heath. I like to take the untrodden path – but I like it like this – cold and a bit drizzly – I like to do it in the rain – in storms even – or snow – I've done it in snow. I almost prefer it to when it's sunny. I feel cheated if it's sunny.

Eddie They said there might be a storm today – later on . . .

Jacklyn That won't stop me! I always like to go for a walk around the equinoxes – especially the beginning of the winter. I think it's such a magical time, Halloween. Intense. The gates are wide open and the dead can walk among the living! I love all that!

She laughs

You're Eddie, aren't you?

Eddie (*uneasy*) Yes.

Jacklyn I heard you chatting to one of the others on the last ramble. You were talking about – well, it doesn't really matter. I just felt like I knew you already – in a weird sort of way. I don't suppose you'd even noticed me?

Eddie (*stuttering*) No, no, no, no, not at all – I mean, I had . . . I certainly was aware – of you.

Jacklyn I'm Jacklyn, by the way, but most people call me Jack.

Eddie smiles. A pause.

So the thing is – I've got this really strong sense that you should – that we should – I mean I very much like to go on instinct – it's the only way I know how to be, in fact – I know you probably think I'm a bit – I don't normally do it this way round – but I felt I should be a little bit brave and see if you'd like to take me out for a drink. No pressure! Just a one-off sort of thing. But if you don't want to, that's fine.

Pause.

Sometimes I'm just too open for my own good.

Eddie Is this a joke?

Jacklyn TRICK OR TREAT?!

She laughs very loudly. Eddie is confused.

No, no. It's not. It's not a joke. I've tried the internet and it only ended in tears. You never know what you're getting. Whereas this way – face-to-face – it's more honest, don't you think?

Eddie (*unsure*) Yes.

Pause.

Jacklyn So?

Eddie Yes. When did you want to –?

Jacklyn It's up to you. I'm free, basically – I have a few evening courses but they're over generally by eight.

Pause.

Eddie What about tonight?

Jacklyn Oh! Steady on, tiger! No. No. That sounds – fine.

Eddie Where did you want to –?

Jacklyn I think you should choose. Since I've done all the legwork. That can be your bit.

Eddie I'll have a think.

Jacklyn That's sorted then! I've got a feeling we're going to have a nice time. No pressure though! I'll give you my card. (*She gives him a card.*) Sounds so professional, doesn't it? I'm training to be a Reiki master.

Eddie looks at the card

It's got my mobile on it . . .

Eddie Thanks.

Jacklyn So you can ring me with a venue and if I don't hear from you, I'll know I've totally freaked you out.

She laughs very loudly.

Eddie No, no, I'll ring you. It was brave of you. To notice me. Thank you.

Jacklyn You're right. I am brave.

Pause.

See you then, Eddie? And keep your neck warm.

Eddie zips his parka up further. She walks off. Eddie stands there a moment, looking at the card. He then puts it into his plastic bag and heads off. Max re-enters. We are back in real time.

Max Eddie?

He sees that Eddie is gone.

You seek him here. You seek him there.

There is a crackle of interference on the TV. Max notices that the it is on, even though there is as yet no picture.

Aha! Playing hard to get.

He picks up the remote control. Reads.

Tuner button. That's the baby.

He starts to tune the television. We see ghostly fleeting images – faces that are not recognisable. Suddenly we are in the wood again and we see a girl of about ten, running happily through the trees. She looks towards the camera, sticks her tongue out. She runs in and out of the trees, looking for a hiding place. She keeps bobbing her head out from behind the trees. Max is transfixed by the image. Suddenly she sees the large yew tree that we saw fleetingly before, it is hollow inside. We see her step inside, she waves at someone behind her – someone we can't see. She is excited by her hiding place.

Unheard dialogue: Girl, 'Look, over here! Over here! This one!'

The girl peeps her head out and beckons towards the other (out of sight) child to join her.

Max (*shocked*) Anna?

He is upset by this turn of events. Abruptly he switches off the TV set. The image on the screen fades

SCENE THREE

Interior: restaurant. Earlier the same day. We hear music quietly – a current chart hit – and the noise of a busy restaurant. The lighting state has changed.

Max stands there looking out. Imogen Cumberbatch enters. She is in her mid-twenties and thirty-eight weeks pregnant. She is a plain girl. She sees Max and goes up to him.

Imogen Mr Villiers? Mr Villiers!

Max Yes?

Max looks at her strangely.

Imogen Imogen Randall. Anna's friend from school.

Max Imogen. Yes. Yes, I know. I'm sorry. I was – that's so strange – I was thinking about Anna – I was just thinking about Anna and then seeing you – I wasn't sure where I was for a minute. Hello, darling. How lovely. Haven't you filled out?

Imogen I'm thirty-eight weeks pregnant.

Max Yes. My God, you really are obscenely pregnant.

Imogen It's driving me mad. Don't tell anyone but I'm wearing men's size-nine shoes. The shame of it.

Max So who's the bugger who did it to you? Do you want me to sort him out?

Imogen You haven't changed! I knew it was you. You're exactly the same except just a bit greyer. Is Mrs Villiers here?

Max No, no, I'm here to meet a client.

Imogen How exciting.

Max Tabby Morris!

Imogen Who's she?

Max Well, it doesn't really – she's a glamour model. She's on the front of – most of the men's magazines – most of the time. It's a hard life, being a writer.

Imogen Oh, I bet Marcus has heard of her. Marcus is my husband – I'm meeting him here for lunch, while we've still got the energy.

Max I don't know, up the duff and married too. The madness of youth. Where have the years gone, Ms Randall?

Imogen Mrs Cumberbatch to you!

Max Mrs Cumberbatch, you proud beauty! I remember you when you were standing in goal – magnificent in orthodontic braces and thigh-high pads. I was terrified of you.

Imogen Oh dear! That sounds awful. It's so funny you saying that about Anna and then me bumping into you like this because I got an e-mail from her today.

Max (*an almost imperceptible tightening*) From Anna?

Imogen Yes! It must be something in the ether! Just this morning I got it. I was shocked, to tell the truth. I think it was just to wish me luck for the baby. You know. She's got so much on her plate and to still remember me.

Max (*trying to be light*) What did she say?

Imogen Oh God, not much. You know what she's like.

Max You should sit down, Imogen. Take the weight off your size-nines.

Imogen Marcus'll be here in a minute.

Max No. No. I insist.

Max sits her on the sofa.

Imogen It is hot in here.

Max We haven't heard from her in a little while. Anna.

Imogen You can never pin her down.

Max No.

Imogen She was so sweet about the baby, like she was genuinely excited which I'm sure she's not. I don't know why she suddenly thought of me. What brought that on?

Max I'm sure she thinks of you all the time. Her best friend from school.

Imogen She doesn't.

Slight pause.

Anyway. She said she was thinking of leaving.

Max What?

Imogen Where is she again?

Max Ramallah.

Imogen I've got a head like a sieve. It is right what they say about your brain shrinking.

Max Is she coming home?

Imogen I don't think so. Haven't you heard from her?

Max What exactly did she say?

Imogen I only read it quickly.

Max She said she was thinking of leaving Ramallah?

Imogen Yes. She said the situation was changing so rapidly and she thought she could do more elsewhere. I think.

Max Where?

Imogen Maybe you should ring her or something?

Max She doesn't like – we don't like to bother her too much.

Imogen I can't remember exactly – somewhere else bad. I can't believe she hasn't told you! Maybe it isn't that fixed.

Max Somewhere else bad?

Imogen starts to fan herself.

Imogen Yes, you know, one of those Amnesty sort of places?

Max Zimbabwe? Darfur? Chechnya? Nepal? Tibet? Romney fucking Marshes? Where?

Imogen Erm. I wasn't really . . . I read it so quickly – I'm not very political. Sorry.

Imogen is breathing slowly and loudly.

Max No. No. Not at all. Just a bit of a . . . I don't know what it is about today but I've got the strangest – I feel as if she's about to walk through that door. Anna. We haven't seen her for nearly two years, but I've got the strongest sense of her – her face – and then seeing you here – it's just odd – are you all right?

Imogen Heartburn.

Max I'll get you some water.

Imogen No – no –

Max I feel terrible now – I've stressed you out – and you in your condition. What can I say? I'm a bastard. You'll have to report me to the social services.

Imogen It's fine – it's going. I'm fine. Look. You're obviously upset about this, so why don't we just pop round to yours tonight?

Max What?

Imogen Me and Marcus. I'd love you two to meet.

Max Well –

Imogen Soon we won't be able to get out. Are you still at the same address?

Max Yes.

Imogen I used to be at yours all the time. It was like a second home to me.

Max About tonight. It's rather short notice.

Imogen I could print up the e-mail. Just pop it round to show you. How about that? That'd clear it all up, wouldn't it? Solve the mystery.

Max I'd have to check with Harriet.

Imogen Oh, she won't need to go to any trouble. We'll only stay an hour. Just for drinks. And I'm not even drinking!

Max Harriet's a perfectionist.

Imogen I think it's always better not to plan. Just to be spontaneous. Then you don't worry.

Max Harriet likes to worry –

Imogen I think Anna getting in touch today – and you and me meeting – I think it's a sign, don't you?

Max Of what exactly?

Imogen Maybe it's because it's Halloween! Spooky!

She laughs.

Max We'd love to have you round. You and Mr Cumberbatch. But properly. You must come properly. For dinner. Another night.

Imogen (*indicating her belly*) I'm afraid I've got a bit of a prior engagement. It's an informal thing, Mr Villiers. No pressure. We could just talk about Anna. Because once the baby comes – I won't have any time – to think about Anna. We'll come early though and leave early. Promise. I'm bursting for the loo. No bladder control. I'd better go – I'm meeting Marcus in the restaurant bit. What do you say, about seven?

She gets up with some difficulty. He helps her.

Max Fabulous.

The music changes in the background to the introduction to Sam Cooke, 'What a Wonderful World'.

Imogen nods and exits. Max stands a moment miserably, looking at her exiting form.

SCENE FOUR

Abrupt lighting change. Interior: lounge.

Max turns and picks up another of the remote controls. He points it towards the stereo. He turns up the volume on the music. Music: Sam Cooke, 'What a Wonderful World', as before. He picks up his can from earlier. Harriet enters. She is absently carrying a large carving knife.

Harriet What time are they coming?

He does not answer, reverently listening to the music as he is.

Max?

Max I think it's the simplicity of his phrasing. The sheer bloody effortlessness. The way he talks his story. He hooks you. Invites you in. But doesn't try too hard. And the belief. That's it – the belief. Sam Cooke, he does not lie.

He sings to her – the three-line chorus from Sam Cooke's 'What a Wonderful World'.

He takes her hand. She lets him for a moment, then picks up the remote control and switches it off.

Harriet Please don't.

Max Harriet?

Harriet Sam Cooke always depresses me. What time are they coming?

Max notices the huge knife in her hands.

Max Let's remain calm about this. It's only drinks.

Harriet (*looking at the knife*) I bought a pumpkin. Thought I'd get into the spirit. I'm not sure why. I've got the top off but I can't get all the stuff out.

Max Open-heart surgery on a pumpkin. Tricky. Do you think it'll pull through?

Harriet I've drawn a scary face but I really need a small knife with a serrated edge. Something I can gouge out the eyes with.

Max How very Shakespearean.

Harriet It's quite satisfying, somehow. I haven't done it for years. Not since –

Max No.

A sad beat between them.

Harriet What time are they coming?

Max Seven, I think she said.

She takes the can of beer from him.

Harriet You've got a lot to do. Tidy up. You need to mull some wine. They're your guests.

She goes to go.

Max I invited Eddie too.

She turns back, looks at him.

You're fond of him really.

Harriet Absence makes the heart fond.

Max He's not here now.

Harriet (*smiling*) Are you sure? He tends to merge.

Max He's lonely.

Harriet (*an edge*) No – I am the one who is lonely, Max. Have you got the TV working yet?

Max It's got a mind of its own.

Pause. They both stare at it.

We didn't have a set for years.

She turns to get the remote controls.

Harriet I'm sure I can do it.

He stops her.

Max Why don't we sit and talk about all the things we never talk about?

Harriet What things?

Max I don't know. You tell me.

Harriet There's nothing to tell.

Max Please.

Pause. She looks at him.

Harriet Okay. I'll tell you about my day.

Max I don't mean that.

Harriet What?

Max I mean important things.

Harriet My day is not important?

Max I know about your day. You brought a rug home. I don't want to hear about your commercial transactions. Tell me what you're thinking. Right now.

Harriet You shouldn't ask me that, not when I'm holding a knife.

Pause.

Max I was thinking about Anna today.

Harriet When are you not thinking about Anna?

Max What's wrong?

Harriet What's wrong? I've had an incredibly stressful day and I come home and find you've invited strangers –

Max Stressful? You bought a rug. You went out and bought a rug. How hard can that be?

Harriet I've told you already, I didn't buy it.

Max That must have been very difficult for such a talented shopper as you. I don't know how you're still managing to stand up –

Harriet You're very unkind to me, Max –

Max Why don't we ring them up now – immediately – give them your credit card details . . .?

Harriet I'm not talking about the rug.

Max You need some perspective, darling. Our daughter is in the West Bank standing in front of bulldozers and you are having a little bit of shopper's guilt. Now which sounds stressful to you? Be honest?

Harriet You always do this – you compare me all the time to Anna – how small my life is in comparison. Why do you do that?

Max Come on, let's ring the shop – put your mind at ease. Maybe they'll give us a discount for cash?

Harriet You could have rung me – to see if it was convenient to invite strangers –

Max Not strangers. A schoolfriend of Anna's – someone we have known since she was eleven years old.

Harriet I know how it goes. You had your sexy little interview with the page-three girl –

Max This is what this is about.

Harriet There you were, a bit pissed with a hard-on the size of Concorde – a supersonic erection – ready to fly but sadly never will again – and ooh! here's another little girly – wink, wink, hello, darling, all the girls fancy me, even the young ones. 'Come round for drinks, Imogen,' standing a little bit too close –

Max She's nine months pregnant –

Harriet How do you know so much about it?

Max You are seriously fucking mad. Imogen Randall. We are talking about Imogen Randall? Who weighed more than me by the age of eight. Who has the face of a troll.

Harriet Face it. The Tabby Morrisses of this world ain't gonna look at you any more. I don't care though, Max. I am not the person who cares any more. I ABSOLVE YOU OF ALL GUILT. It's the talk – all your talk I find so wearying. All the fucking elaboration that goes on. That gets us exactly nowhere. Don't you realise – the truth lies in what is not said, Max? I just – want you to – mull – the – wine. For our guests. Yes?

She hands him the knife. He grips her hand tightly – the knife between them, before taking it.

The wine?

Max Will be well and truly mulled.

Max exits with the knife. Harriet looks momentarily stricken.

Harriet Today I brought home a rug. That's all I did. Nothing else.

Slowly she kneels on the rug.

SCENE FIVE

Interior, rug shop. Earlier the same day. Harriet is kneeling – the light and the atmosphere feels almost spiritual. Burak enters – he is a good-looking, gentle, intelligent Turkish man in his early thirties.

Burak Mrs Villiers?

She goes to get up.

Harriet I'm sorry, I was just –

Burak Please – be my guest.

She smiles at him. Kneels back down.

Harriet This is a new one.

Burak Today I display it.

Harriet Tell me about it.

Burak East Anatolian, probably. A copy of a much older design but an antique in its own right. Wool on cotton. It is an unusual texture though.

He turns the corner over for her.

You see – the tightly packed knotting allows virtually no weft to be seen. The colours are still good . . . and typically Kurdish – indigo, henna, saffron and forest green – the traditional vegetable dyes.

Harriet (*smiling*) Yes.

Burak The motif is also traditional – the tree of life. You see heaven and earth are connected by the tree which grows at the earth's centre. The spirit must climb through the various levels of branches on its way to heaven. From each branch you see the hanging-candle motifs symbolising the holy, eternal flame. It was probably a prayer rug although it is unusually large. The devotional motifs seem to indicate a spiritual purpose.

Harriet traces the tree's trunk.

Harriet I think this may be the one, Burak.

Burak I leave you to enjoy it.

Harriet How much is it?

Burak pauses, sighs.

Burak Three thousand.

Harriet I'm just worried it might be too big for my sitting room. Could you give me the measurements?

Burak Of course.

Harriet Mind you, I think it'll be fine – big is good, isn't it? I wouldn't want it too small.

Burak Mrs Villiers –

Harriet It's not too green?

Burak Mrs Villiers –

Harriet What?

Burak You have been coming in my shop ever since it opened. Six months.

Harriet It's a beautiful shop.

Burak You have looked at every rug I have. I have laid them before you. You have considered each one in turn. You have been appreciative. But each one has been dismissed – too large, too small, too old, too new, the colours wrong, the colours right but the shape wrong –

Harriet I know – I'm sorry –

Burak Believe me, I know it is a difficult purchase to make. It is a lot of money. Some rugs tug at your heart but not your head. And as eager as I am to sell – I am a businessman, after all – I feel these rugs are important. They have value beyond their price.

Harriet I agree completely.

Burak You are a nice woman and I am a patient man, but I have shown you everything I have. You come back and you come back – sometimes twice, three times in one week. You say, 'This is the one,' and 'I have made my decision,' then, 'Just show me the first rug I ever looked at again' –

Harriet But I think *this is* the one – I really do.

Burak You trouble me, Mrs Villiers. I lie in bed and I think of you. I think, 'What can I show her next?' 'What does she really want?' 'What will please her?' And then it comes to me. In a flash. You know what I think, Mrs Villiers?

Harriet What?

Burak You do not want a rug.

Harriet I do.

Burak (*emphatic*) You don't.

Harriet I do.

Burak No.

Harriet (*sadly*) I thought I did.

Burak Don't get me wrong – you are free to come back and browse – I am used to your company now. It would seem strange if you did not come, but you do not have to buy a rug. Please. Let me free you from the obligation because, to be honest, I feel the pressure too. My instinct is to make the sale and I see now that it will not happen, so let us relieve ourselves of this burden. You will not buy a rug. There. Deal?

Harriet I'm not sure –

Burak I feel a weight has lifted already.

Harriet I can get some cash out if it's easier.

Burak No.

Harriet Please don't say that.

Burak Let it go.

He moves away. She does not move. He stops as she speaks.

Harriet (*out of control, breathless*) You will sell me this rug. Do you hear me? Don't you walk away from me. I'm not leaving without this rug. I want this fucking rug.

Burak You should go now –

Harriet I'm not going. Who do you think you are? You don't know anything about me. You think you know me? Think you can see straight through me? You know nothing about me. Nothing at all –

Burak Mrs Villiers, stop this –

Harriet Look at me. I know who I am. I want things, all right? I'm not ashamed of that. That's how I live now. I want all the things I can touch and hold – all the things – I want to surround myself with beautiful things. So that I don't have to see the fucking squalor everywhere, all right?

Burak There is no need for this.

Harriet This is where I live. These four corners. You don't understand. This rug is my right. It is my hope and my anchor. That's what I want. That's all I want. You can't deny me that. No one can deny me that. Please God.

She puts her head on the rug. She is crying. He sits next to her.

Burak Perhaps you should not seek to be anchored.

Harriet looks at him.

You have a beautiful face.

Harriet What?

Burak There is one thing I forgot to tell you about this rug. It is magic. With this you can fly. Right up the tree to the top.

Harriet When can you deliver?

Suddenly she leans over and kisses him. They stop, look at each other and then kiss more passionately. He pushes her down on the rug, lies on top of her. She abandons herself to the moment. He stops.

Burak I shut up shop, yes?

Harriet Yes.

He gets up, exits. Harriet lies there a moment. She speaks softly.

I do not belong on the ground.

SCENE SIX

Interior: lounge. The doorbell goes. Lighting change.

Max (*off*) I'll get it.

Harriet gets up and exits upstairs just as Imogen enters the room followed by Max. Imogen carries a bottle of water.

Imogen What a beautiful rug! Gosh.

Max Harriet can't decide whether to keep it.

Imogen Oh no! It's a real statement.

Max What does it say exactly? To you.

Imogen Oh. I don't know. I just meant –

Max I know what it says to me, and it involves far too many noughts.

Imogen I think you should definitely keep it. Where is Mrs Villiers?

Max She'll be down in a minute.

Imogen She didn't – mind us coming round at such short notice?

Max She's thrilled. Did you bring the e-mail?

Imogen Oh God! I knew there was something.

She sits.

But it's okay. It's Burma.

Max What?

Imogen She's going to Burma. Apparently things are really bad there.

Max Burma.

Imogen I don't know where it is. Burma. Do you?

Marcus enters. He is an attractive man of about thirty – straight as a die, methodical, decent, upright. He jangles his car keys in his hand.

Marcus I found a space.

Imogen Well done.

Marcus Just down the street. It says residents' parking till six. I wasn't sure if it applied to the whole street?

Max It does. As a resident I can confirm this.

Marcus Opposite the entrance to the private gardens I am.

Max Perfect. You've found your space. You occupy it.

Marcus I agree with parking restrictions in principle, just don't like to be caught out. Oh bugger. Imo, I forgot your cushions. Do you want me to go back?

Imogen No, I'm fine.

Marcus Are you sure? I don't mind.

Max I'm sure we can rustle up some cushions. My wife does cushions. It's one of her chief accomplishments . . . We have totally pointless cushions everywhere. You should see our bed. It takes me half the night to find the actual pillows under the mountains of extraneous cushionage.

Imogen I'm fine anyway, Marcus. Stop fussing!

Max Now how about some wine?

Imogen I'll stick to the water.

Marcus (*to Imogen*) Are you sure you want to drive later? Because I can just as easily –

Imogen I'll drive.

Max We're all set then. I'll go and get the wine.

Imogen Sorry. Mr Villiers –

Max Max, please.

Imogen Can you just tell me where the loo is? Baby's pressing on my bladder.

Max Upstairs. First door on the right . . .

Imogen puts her water down and exits. Marcus wanders downstage and looks at the 'screen'.

Marcus I want one of these.

Max Ah yes.

Marcus Nice piece of kit. Looks good.

Max The black is deeper than on any other plasma TV.

Marcus What's the picture like?

Max It's . . . very real. Although I'm having trouble with terrestrial at the moment.

Marcus Nice.

Max Just a few teething problems.

Marcus I'm going to wait till they come down in price.

Max Good plan.

The doorbell goes. Marcus turns away from the screen. Suddenly the screen pings into action of its own accord. We see the wood again. We zoom in on the ancient yew tree. We see the young Anna running around the tree – chasing another child who is not visible. She has a stick in her hand. Her mood is light.

Unheard dialogue: Anna, 'I'm going to get you! I'm coming to get you!'

Max goes white. He is deeply shocked.

Marcus I'm afraid we won't be able to stay very long.

Max (*in response to the screen*) Oh God.

Marcus Imogen gets very tired.

Max is still reacting to the screen. The little girl is now running in circles around the trees as if the other child were chasing her. She is laughing.

Max Oh my God.

Marcus looks at him, and then the screen.

Marcus Are you okay?

Max frantically pushes the button on the remote control, trying to rid the screen of this image. It is clear Marcus cannot see what is going on.

What? Do you want to turn it on?

The doorbell goes again. The image fades. He puts the remote control down.

Max No, no. Sorry. Bloody thing. I'm fine. Fine. Harriet? Darling? Can you get that? What were you saying?

Marcus Imogen gets tired very quickly.

Max Does she? Good. Good. I'll just go and get the drinks. Make yourself at home.

Max exits. Marcus looks at the screen, frowns.

Lighting change. The screen returns to the image we had for the restaurant earlier.

SCENE SEVEN

As the lighting changes we flashback to the restaurant from earlier. Sound and lightscape as before. Music plays and we hear people chatting, etc. Imogen enters with heartburn.

Marcus (*still frowning*) Where've you been? I've only got an hour.

Imogen I'm sorry –

Marcus I've had to order mine. I haven't really got time for this.

Imogen Heartburn.

Marcus Sit down. Have my water.

He picks up the water and gives it to her. She drinks.

Something just happened.

Imogen What?

Marcus There was an incident by the shops. This woman stepped out in front of a car.

Imogen Oh my God.

Marcus Just stepped out. I had to grab her. Not paying any attention. Didn't go to the pedestrian crossing which was only a hundred yards away. Stepped out between two parked vehicles – they were people carriers, a Citroën and a Hyundai – the motorist wouldn't have seen her. Luckily I was there and I had my wits about me. I saw her out of the corner my eye and anticipated it all. Just a split-second thing. But I managed to pull her back. She could have been killed.

Imogen My goodness. What did she say?

Marcus Nothing. Nothing at all. She looked at me in the strangest way and then she just walked off. Went into the greengrocer's as if nothing had happened.

Imogen How old was she?

Marcus Middle-aged? I don't know.

Imogen She didn't thank you?

Marcus No.

Imogen Must have been embarassed.

Marcus I feel a bit shaken up by it. The way she looked at me.

Imogen People are so ungrateful.

Marcus She would have been killed. I did react very quickly. I think it's because of the baby. I'm ready. You know. I feel ready.

Imogen I know.

Marcus I *was* quick. To catch her like that. Grabbed her round the waist. Sort of rugby-tackled her onto the Lexus boot. Hurt my wrist a bit.

Imogen Poor you.

Marcus I'm shaking. Look.

Imogen It was brave of you.

Marcus (*troubled*) Mmm. Yes.

Imogen I don't think I'll eat . . . the heartburn . . . not if you're in a rush.

Marcus You need to eat, Imo.

Imogen I'll get something at home. I just met Anna's dad.

Marcus Who's Anna?

Imogen From school. You know. (*Annoyed.*) Marcus.

Marcus Was she at the wedding?

Imogen No, she couldn't come – she was in Israel, remember?

Marcus The activist?

Imogen Yes. Anyway, I just met her dad. I've known her parents since I was little. He's a bit annoying. Thinks he's a bit funnier than he actually is. Anyway, he's invited us round for drinks.

Marcus Good job we've got the baby excuse.

Imogen Thing is – he seemed a bit depressed – so I sort of said yes. I said we'd just pop round for an hour tonight –

Marcus You'll have to cancel.

Imogen I can't do that. It would be mean. I've got his hopes up. I'll have to go by myself –

Marcus How can you go by yourself? Look at you.

Imogen It's a real pain, I know. I don't want to go. It's the last thing I want. But I feel I ought to.

Marcus I can see I'm going to have to put my foot down.

Imogen I owe it to her. To go.

Marcus You could go after the baby –

Imogen (*vehement*) No! I don't want to go after the baby. I want to go today!

Marcus What are you talking about?

Imogen Anna and I were very close. She is risking her life out there. It's the least I can do. For her family.

Marcus All right, all right, keep your hair on. We can go. Though you really should be resting.

Imogen I know. But the change of scene might help me sleep better.

Marcus sighs.

Marcus (*annoyed, looking around*) Is anyone going to bring me a drink?

The doorbell goes. Lighting change. Music off.

SCENE EIGHT

Max re-enters with a bowl of mulled wine with glasses attached to it.

Max Mulled wine, Mr Cumberbatch? Or I've got red wine or whisky if you'd prefer.

Marcus Whisky, please. I'm not a fan of cinnamon.

Max puts the wine down. He opens a concealed door in the bark wall which reveals a drinks cabinet.

Max Harriet's on her way.

During the following he pours whisky for Marcus and opens some red wine for himself.

We've got another couple of guests coming. Eddie. A schoolfriend of mine, in fact. Funny how school friendships run deep. You and Anna – me and Eddie. It's like Friends Reunited tonight. We'll probably all end up filing for divorce.

Imogen You know I think I'll just have a small glass. I love mulled wine.

Marcus Are you sure?

Max It's good for 'baby'. Happy Halloween.

At this Harriet enters. She has changed. She wears an expensive black dress and high shoes. She looks beautiful, ethereal. She carries the pumpkin reverently: it has a ghoulish face and a candle inside. They all stop at her entrance. She places it carefully on a branch/ ledge. Marcus looks at her oddly. But they are all a little under her spell in this moment.

Harriet There. Keep the demons away.

Max Perfect timing, darling.

Imogen Mrs Villiers.

Harriet *(all charm)* Don't be silly, Imogen, darling. Call me Harriet. We're all grown-ups here. And look how grown up you are now. About to be a mummy, too – you're far too young. Congratulations, sweetheart. And is this Daddy?

She looks at Marcus. A flicker of recognition, and then she is all charm again. He is slightly ill at ease.

Imogen Marcus Cumberbatch, my husband.

He puts out his hand. She leans forward and kisses him on the cheek.

Harriet Hello, Marcus Cumberbatch.

Marcus (*uneasy*) Pleased to meet you.

Harriet Yes . . . I wish my Anna had found someone like you, Marcus Cumberbatch. That would have stopped her gallivanting off around the world. Sit down, Imogen. Can I get you a footstool?

Imogen No, no, really.

Harriet You should keep your feet up or else you'll swell.

Imogen I'm already in men's size-nines. I'm a real clodhopper these days.

Harriet Take your shoes off.

Imogen I'm fine.

Harriet It's just I have to be a little bit careful – with the rug.

Max Let her clodhop, darling, for goodness sake.

Harriet I might have to take it back. It's not paid for.

Marcus We can take our shoes off.

Imogen I'm not sure I can reach mine.

Marcus (*snapping*) I'll do it. Don't bend, Imogen! What did the doctor say?

He takes her shoes off for her.

Max What exactly is this rug for, Harriet, if not to tread upon?

Harriet It's delicate.

Max Then hang it on the wall.

Harriet Perhaps I could cover up that mammothly ugly screen with it.

Marcus (*indicating his shoes*) Mine are clean.

Max And what about your spikes, dear?

Harriet I'm sorry, I'm neurotic. Put them back on for God's sake, Imogen.

Imogen Oh.

Max You really should have provided some moccasins for our guests, Harriet.

Harriet It's just I haven't paid for the rug yet –

Imogen It's actually more comfortable. I should let my feet breathe.

Harriet You see. Imogen's feet are breathing. Are you all right, Marcus?

Marcus Splendid.

Harriet Marcus *is* splendid, I can tell. I, however, am dying of thirst.

Max Mulled wine, darling?

Harriet Oh! What a good idea, Max! Something warming.

   Pause.

Marcus Your daughter's in Israel then, Harriet?

Harriet That's right.

Marcus What exactly is she doing there?

Harriet She's missing out on all the eligible young men, that's what she's doing.

Imogen I doubt that.

Max She's a member of the International Solidarity Movement.

Marcus Like that girl who died?

Max That's right.

Imogen Which girl?

Marcus She was killed by the IDF. Allegedly.

Max (*wanting to change the subject*) Who was at the door?

Harriet Some children. All dressed up. I didn't have anything for them. I should have thought. I don't keep sweet things in the house. In the end I found some Savoiardi biscuits we bought last year in France. I'm pretty sure they're stale. You should have seen their disappointed faces . . . Now I want to hear all about this little one.

She goes to Imogen, indicates her belly.

Imogen Do you want to have a feel?

Harriet Oh! No – really –

Imogen (*taking her hand*) Here. He's kicking. Can you feel?

Harriet Oh my gosh. Yes. Yes. (*She pulls her hand away. A little shaken.*) What a strange sensation.

Max (*concerned*) Harriet?

Harriet I don't remember ever being this big. Do you think I was this big?

Max It was a long time ago.

Harriet Do you know what it is?

Imogen We didn't want to know.

Marcus I think it's a boy!

Harriet A boy. Lovely.

Imogen I didn't enjoy the scans. They say the baby has a one in two hundred chance of being Down's Syndrome, which is a very bad result, apparently, especially considering my age –

Marcus Imo –

Imogen Marcus wanted to have all the tests done, but there's a risk of miscarriage. I think it's better to believe that the baby will be okay. I feel very positive about it.

Max It'll be fine. More than fine.

Imogen (*snappy*) What does that mean? I mean, it doesn't matter if it's Down's Syndrome, does it?

Marcus Of course not. But it won't be.

Harriet Have you chosen a name?

Imogen We can't agree on one.

Max The baby already has the fine name of Cumberbatch. A name to conjure with.

Marcus It means 'dweller in a valley with a stream'.

Max How gratifyingly specific.

Marcus I get asked a lot about it. Being an unusual name. There are a lot of Cumberbatches in North Staffordshire.

Harriet Did you grow up there?

Marcus No. I'm from Surrey.

The doorbell goes.

Harriet We're going to be plagued tonight. I've got nothing for them. Perhaps we should just ignore it.

Max They don't want sweets, anyway, they want lattes and heroin.

Imogen It's a really beautiful rug, Mrs Villiers. I was just admiring it before you came down.

Harriet Thank you.

Imogen I always remember your house being beautiful. Anna used to get sick of me going on about it. There was always something new to look at. Every time I came, the furniture had all been moved around and there was a new sofa or kitchen or something.

Harriet (*laughing*) You're exaggerating.

Max She's not.

Harriet My husband derides me for the pride I take in appearances. For the time I take to make our home more comfortable. He would like us to revert to living like savages.

Marcus We need to move.

Max Harriet has become increasingly epicurean in her old age. She was totally unmaterialistic when I met her. It was all music festivals and long flowing hair.

Harriet He loved me when I was a hippy –

Max But now her head is constantly turned by the cheap glitter of objects.

Harriet On the contrary – I find inherent spirituality in objects. Take Imogen's shoes –

Imogen Please don't – I think they smell.

Harriet (*ignoring her*) I find Imogen's shoes very poignant. The size of them, the width, and here you can see the imprint of her toes. Without any feet in them, they look forlorn.

Max Without any feet in them they cease to be useful. Objects should function. Full stop.

Harriet The beauty of an object has nothing to do with its utility.

Max (*to Marcus*) My wife is very beautiful, don't you think?

Marcus Um, yes. She has a face – one remembers.

Max Yes.

He smiles at Harriet, who turns to Imogen.

Harriet (*to Imogen*) Your shoe, Cinders.

Imogen Ugly Sister, more like!

Marcus We just need more space.

Max In my experience space is always filled. Almost immediately you will yearn for more space. And then more. You will never be happy.

Eddie enters, followed by Jacklyn. Eddie has not changed although he's taken his parka off. Jacklyn wears flowing black and purple hippy clothes and resembles a witch.

Eddie I used the key you lent me.

Max Ah Eddie, my first love! Welcome.

Eddie Sorry, Harriet. We did ring.

Harriet You've got a key? You gave him a key?

Max Of course I gave him a key.

Eddie This is Jacklyn.

Max Well, well, well, Eddie you dark horse. Very pleased to meet you, Jacklyn.

Harriet is looking dumbfounded.

Jacklyn Most people call me Jack.

Max Well, Jack – how fabulous. And you've come in costume too!

Jacklyn I haven't.

Eddie She hasn't come in costume.

Max No, of course not. I was tricking you. Come in, come in, sit down. No – introductions, introductions. This is Imogen, a friend of our daughter's –

The dialogue overlaps at this point.

Imogen Hello!

Jacklyn (*seeing her bump, a fraction uneasily*) Oh, look at you. You haven't got long –

Imogen Two weeks –

Jacklyn A little Scorpian!

Max – and her husband, Marcus.

Eddie Hello, Marcus.

Marcus I didn't catch your –

Eddie Eddie. Eddie.

Max Eddie and Jacklyn. And my wife, Harriet.

Jacklyn Thank you for inviting me.

Harriet (*surprised*) Yes.

Max Superb. Let me get you drinks.

Harriet is looking dumbfounded. Max hands out drinks. Imogen takes more wine.

Harriet Eddie?

Eddie Harriet.

Harriet This is not – you are not –

Eddie Say it, Harriet.

Harriet Is this your *girlfriend*?

Jacklyn Oh no, no, nothing like that.

Eddie We're friends.

Jacklyn We met rambling.

Max I bet you're a right little rambler, Jack.

Jacklyn laughs.

Harriet I'm in a state of shock.

Max Harriet – can you behave –

Eddie No, let her get it off her chest, Max.

Harriet Did you know about this – ?

Max Not exactly.

Harriet I have known you for twenty-five years, Eddie Fox, and you have never to my knowledge had a girlfriend –

Eddie I didn't realise I needed your dispensation, Harriet.

Max Come on, give him a chance, he was in a monastery for some of those years.

Jacklyn You were in a monastery?

Eddie Briefly.

Harriet He was a Carthusian monk, locked away in a cell, Jacklyn! If that doesn't make him a homosexual, I don't know what does!

Eddie I'm not a homosexual –

Max He's not a homosexual. He styles his hair with yoghurt, for God's sake. The homosexuals are a stylish lot, Eddie, they wouldn't look twice at you. No offence, mate.

Eddie None taken.

Harriet Well, I'm pretty sure he's never knowingly dipped his wick –

Max Harriet!

Eddie It's all right, Max. It's all jealousy. You know you want me, Harriet. Just say it.

Harriet You leave me speechless, Eddie Fox.

Max You could do a lot worse than Eddie, Jack.

Eddie I apologise for my friends.

Jacklyn It's all right. I like to go on my instinct. And the minute I met Eddie – I had this sense of 'light' from him.

Harriet Well, there you go, then.

Eddie (*to Jacklyn*) Thank you. I think that's the nicest thing anyone has ever said about me.

Jacklyn You're welcome.

Harriet I shall go out tomorrow and buy a hat.

Eddie You won't be invited.

Harriet smiles at him.

Imogen I've never met a monk before.

Marcus Nor me. What's a Carthu . . . ?

Eddie Carthusian. They're a contemplative order. Silent.

Imogen What did you contemplate?

Eddie The immensity of love. Mostly . . .

Pause.

I never took my solemn vows. It was a long time ago now.

Imogen Why did you leave?

Eddie I was too lazy to sit and pray all day.

Harriet Eddie felt he just wasn't spending enough time bumming around at our house. So regrettably he had to leave.

Max Their loss, our gain.

Pause. It grows imperceptibly darker in the room.

Jacklyn We had a lovely walk from the tube. Looking at all the children. Dressed as ghosts and ghouls.

Imogen Ahh!

Eddie Some really tiny ones.

Jacklyn They make me want to cry. The really little ones.

Imogen Oh! I'd love to see them.

Marcus I find it all a bit too commercial.

Max Quite right. A load of American tosh.

Jacklyn Oh no. No. It's very traditional. It all comes from a pagan root.

Eddie Does it?

Jacklyn The pagans believed that for one day in the year time should be completely abolished.

Max Quite right.

Jacklyn We are now officially in 'no time'.

Harriet Is that what it is?

Max You seem to be an authority, Jack.

Jacklyn I've flirted with neo-paganism.

Max Haven't we all?

Jacklyn We're all allowed to be wild tonight. Let off steam, you know. So that order can be re-established tomorrow.

Max Sounds like a very good plan to me.

Jacklyn It's the night when the moon is dark so that our mortal sight can be obscured and we can get a glimpse of the other side.

Max See through a glass darkly.

Eddie The gates are open.

Jacklyn Exactly. But only if we all believe.

Imogen Oh golly.

Jacklyn The spirit world is very near. Like a reflection in a deep, clear pool.

Max looks at the screen.

Max Yes. Yes.

Pause.

Jacklyn 'Hell night', they used to call it.

The doorbell rings. Imogen jumps, startled.

53

Imogen Sorry. It made me jump.

Harriet I don't think it'll work. I'm not sure I'm a believer. Sorry.

Jacklyn Whether you believe or not, I think it pays to listen to the spirit world.

Max opens the drinks cupboard.

Max (*pouring himself a whisky*) I am forever open to the spirit world. Here's to hell night! A night of hell.

Harriet That's comfortingly familiar for us, Max.

The doorbell rings again. The TV flickers for a moment. We see a fleeting image of the ancient yew tree. Only Max sees it. It disappears. He takes a swift drink.

Jacklyn I suppose it's all about death really, isn't it?

Imogen Oh dear.

Jacklyn Confronting death in some way.

Imogen Do we have to?

Eddie Yes, that's important. The monks would agree with you there. We all need to confront death.

Imogen That's just so sad.

Marcus I don't think you should drink any more.

Imogen I'm fine. Just a little emotional.

Marcus We should probably think about getting you home.

Imogen No, we shouldn't, thank you very much. You're such a spoilsport sometimes, Marcus.

Marcus I'm only thinking of you.

Imogen I want to propose a toast. To my dear friend

Anna. Who is risking her life in Israel for others. And who is now off to risk her life in Burma – for the Burmese people, who have no idea what's about to hit them. To Anna, who still found the time in her busy, busy schedule to remember dull little me.

Harriet Anna's going to Burma?

Marcus Imo?

Harriet Max?

Max (*evasive*) I was going to –

Harriet What? You've spoken to Anna? And you didn't tell me?

Suddenly the TV screen bounces into life. Max is transfixed by it. He is the only one who sees it. We see the image of a group of children running wildly through a wood. They are laughing, chasing each other. The camera focuses for a moment on the little girl from earlier: she reaches out her hand towards another child whom we don't see. She takes his hand, although we do not see him. We see her running off, away from the camera. The doorbell rings again.

Max Oh God.

Imogen (*raising her glass*) To Anna! Come on everyone!

Harriet Max!

The others hesitantly raise their glasses.

All (*except Harriet*) To Anna!

Harriet Max, what's wrong with you?

Max Look at the screen.

Harriet What are you talking about?

Imogen (*suddenly wincing in pain*) Ow!

Marcus Imo? Imo! What is it?

Max (*looking at the screen*) She can't do it.

Imogen can't speak with the pain. She kneels on the floor, on the rug, trying to catch her breath.

Jacklyn She can do it. We're fine. I'm a trained doula. Just give her some space. You're all right, Imogen.

Jacklyn kneels beside her. The following dialogue overlaps.

Breathe. That's it.

Imogen I'm not ready for this!

The doorbell rings again.

Max (*looking at the screen*) It's Anna.

Harriet What? You're not making any sense. Eddie? You talk to him.

Eddie Max, what is it?

The doorbell rings again.

Max (*more urgently*) It's Anna!

Imogen whimpers with pain again.

Marcus I don't like the look of this. I'm ringing the hospital. I'm going to get your notes.

Marcus runs out.

Imogen I feel sick.

Jacklyn Where's the toilet? Eddie?

Eddie Upstairs.

Harriet Why is she in Burma? What did she say to you? Max, you're not listening to me.

Jacklyn Come on, Imogen.

Eddie I'll show you.

Eddie leads Jacklyn and Imogen out. Max stares at the screen, stricken by what he sees. On the screen there is a storm brewing. The little girl runs towards the tree. She is beckoning for the other child to follow. The trunk is hollow and she steps inside it. We see a close-up of her face. She looks cold and a little scared. The doorbell rings again.

Harriet (*annoyance at the door*) Oh for God's sake! Bloody children. I haven't got anything for you! Go away! Leave us alone.

The doorbell rings again.

Harriet (*leaving, to Max*) I haven't finished with you.

Harriet exits. On the screen Anna speaks to the child we don't see: 'Don't worry, it'll be all right.'

Max No, my Anna. No.

The doorbell continues to ring. Max is left on his own. There is a flash on the screen and the picture fades to interference.

Blackout.

End of Act One.

Act Two

SCENE ONE

The stage is bare. Music: Sam Cooke, 'Bring it on Home to Me'.

Max is alone in the sitting room. He is trying the remote controls again. Eddie enters. He looks at Max.

Max I'm going to take it back. What's the point of having the deepest black in the world when there's no bloody picture?

The doorbell goes. He turns his attention from the screen. Eddie goes to go to the door.

Don't. Stay with me. Harriet can get it. So, anyone busy being born?

Eddie Not here. Not tonight. False alarm.

Max Shame. We've got an old paddling pool in the shed. I was looking forward to getting stuck in. Where are they all?

Eddie Imogen and Jack are in the toilet. Marcus went to his car, I think. Max. Before, you seemed –

Max What?

Eddie I don't know. Shall I get you a beer?

Max I'm fine. I'm fine, but I'm an arsehole and God bless you. God bless you, Eddie Fox.

Eddie Why?

Max Always here.

Eddie Oh dear.

Pause. Max smiles at him. He goes and picks up the opened bottle of red wine and glasses for him and Eddie.

Max You know there was once a very famous Chinese zither player – I don't know where – but for argument's sake let's say China – and he had a friend who was known throughout the land as The Most Famous Listener. It is said that when the friend died, the player cut his strings and refused to play again.

Eddie smiles.

And have you ever heard a Chinese zither? Christ, it's rank. A high-pitched wailing with a simultaneously bass droning quality to it.

Eddie laughs. The doorbell goes. Max looks back at the screen.

Eddie I don't think Harriet could have –

Max No.

Eddie Shall I get it, then?

Max It might be Anna.

Eddie What?

Max That's how it'll be one day. The doorbell will go and she'll be home. Just like that.

Eddie (*worried about him*) Yes. Yes, it will. Definitely. I'll go and check, then.

Max looks back at the screen. Eddie exits. The doorbell goes again.

Max (*rehearsing it*) Hello, Anna.

A lighting change.

SCENE TWO

Interior: restaurant. We are in flashback, in the same restaurant as earlier, so the same sound and lightscape. Tabby Morris enters behind Max. Tabby is a very pretty, blonde girl of twenty-five. She is dressed very demurely – in fact she immediately belies Max's description of her: she is much more Home Counties, much more sunny girl-next-door than we might have expected. She does wear dark glasses that she raises to look for Max. Music plays in the background.

Tabby Hello.

Max swings round. He is still holding the wine bottle.

Max Hello?

Tabby Oh, good. I thought you'd have given up on me. I'm so late – sorry, sorry, sorry. I can't apologise enough –

She looks at him: he appears bewildered.

Tabby – Tabby Morris? Yes? You were expecting me?

Max Yes! I'm sorry. I was just – I just got some bad news. My daughter – I wasn't thinking straight.

Tabby Well, it's been a long time since I wasn't recognised.

Max I'm sorry.

Tabby No. It's bloody nice actually. I need a drink. (*Sitting.*) I'm coming down with a cold and I've got to go to some godforsaken, freezing, in-the-middle-of-nowhere warehouse after this and dress up as Santa's little helper. Fur bikini and real snow apparently. I am not in the Christmas spirit.

Max Well, no, not yet.

Tabby It's not even November. So are you going to pour me some wine?

Max Oh – sorry, I don't know what's wrong with me –

He pours her some wine.

Tabby My agent should have sent you some DVDs and videos and stuff. For research purposes.

Max I got them this morning. I'm afraid I haven't had a chance yet –

She bats this away.

Tabby So how does this work?

Max Well, we meet at a mutually convenient time. You talk. Tell me the facts. I listen. I write it down. Structure it. Send you a chapter. You send me notes. We thrash it out. You approve. I sign over all rights to you. *My Life* by Tabitha Morris. That is, if you think I'm the man for the job.

Tabby Are you the man for the job?

Max I hope so. My wife has expensive taste.

Tabby Fair enough. Well. For a start, I think we'll need a better title.

Max *Tabitha Reveals All.*

Tabby (*self-aware*) I don't do nude. I always insist on a nice pair of shoes.

Max You will be metaphorically well-shod at all times. You won't have to bare anything you don't want to. Least of all your soul.

Tabby I don't want to give it all away.

Max Well, no, quite. There might be a second volume. And a third.

Tabby So I can be whoever I want to be?

Max I'm a magician!

Tabby I've always yearned for an identity.

Max Me too.

Tabby I was speaking to my dad this morning. He said, 'Why do they want to write a book about you? You're only twenty-five – you haven't lived.'

Max There's a lot of people would like to read about your life.

Tabby A lot of pervs.

Max Not at all. You're making a difference to people's lives.

Tabby Am I? Sort of like Florence Nightingale?

Max You're making an impact. That appears to be more important these days.

Tabby I agree with my dad. I'm famous for having surgically enhanced breasts – I don't know how anyone could spin that out to two hundred pages.

Max I'm very good at what I do.

Tabby My poor dad. It's not easy for him. He can't talk to any of his mates without them mentally picturing me in a thong. It's given him ulcers.

Max He must enjoy your success.

Tabby He'd have preferred it if I'd become a doctor.

Max I'm sure he's very proud of you.

Tabby He's proud of my bank balance.

Max Well, there's a chapter for you.

Tabby I want him to forgive me.

Max We all want to be forgiven. Christ, I'm first in the line.

Tabby Don't get me wrong – I don't think I've done anything wrong. I just think he'll feel better if he forgives me and that will make me feel better. That's off the record, obviously.

Max Obviously.

Pause.

Tabby So your daughter –

Max What?

Tabby You said you had a daughter.

Max Yes. I do.

Tabby What's the bad news?

Max The bad news? The bad news is my daughter hates me.

Tabby Okay.

Max Doesn't want to see me. Wants her space. Wants any space in the world that doesn't involve me in it.

Tabby Is she a doctor, then? Your daughter?

Max No. Anna – Anna is a peace activist. She's in Israel at the moment. Standing in front of tanks.

Tabby That must be marginally worse than standing in front of the paparazzi.

Max Anything needs saving, she wants to save it. She's been like it since she was ten years old.

Tabby Fuck.

Max She has turned herself into a human shield.

Tabby I'd love to have morals.

Max They sell them on eBay now.

Tabby Is she your only child?

A tiny pause.

Max Yes.

Tabby You should be writing about her.

Max Anna?

Tabby She sounds like a good subject.

Max We're here to talk about you.

Tabby I don't mind. I'm sick of me. You can talk about me anywhere. Me and my breasts, me and my boyfriend, me and my shopping bags. Every stranger I meet in the street knows more about me than I know myself. In fact I'm the one who needs a human shield.

Max Mmm.

Tabby Are you okay?

Max I miss her. Like a punishment I miss her.

Pause. Max looks as if he might cry.

Tabby Don't give her any space, eh? Tell her to get her arse back here.

She touches him lightly.

Max Thank you.

Tabby What?

Max For being kind. To an old man.

Tabby Don't be stupid.

Max You're not what I expected.

Tabby You mean, thick.

Max No. Your face.

Tabby What about my face?

Max You have the most beautiful face.

Tabby Thank you.

Max Really exquisite.

He reaches out to touch her face.

Tabby (*laughing but unsure*) What are you doing?

He touches her face – holds it, studies it.

Max It's such a young face.

Tabby Don't.

Max An innocent face.

Tabby Max.

Max You remind me of her –

Tabby Stop it.

Max You don't look alike. It's just she's driven like you – but vulnerable, so vulnerable.

Tabby Get your hands off me.

He lets go of her.

Max What?

Tabby You think this is turning me on –

Max No. I didn't mean it like that –

Tabby Nobody touches me, do you understand?

Max I'm sorry – I wasn't trying to –

Tabby You're all the fucking same.

Max I'm sorry – I was thinking of my daughter.

Tabby That's worse! You're fucking sick – I told my agent I wanted a woman to do me –

Max I'm sorry. I don't know what I was thinking. It was unprofessional of me –

Tabby Too fucking right.

Max I'm not normally like this –

Tabby Fucking innocent face. What's that supposed to mean? Think that'll win me over?

Max I'm sorry. I misread the situation.

Tabby You're telling me.

Max I need this job. I do.

Tabby You think I'd have you now? Give you a piece of myself? No way. You know nothing about me. You know nothing at all. And that's the way it's going to stay.

She pulls her sunglasses down.

Max Tabby –

Tabby Miss Morris to you. You know what, I think your daughter's got the right idea.

She gets up and leaves. He watches her go. He drinks some wine.

Lighting change. Interior: sitting room. Harriet enters.

Harriet What the fuck's going on?

Max (*startled*) Christ, Harriet.

Harriet Will you tell me exactly what's going on?

Max I haven't spoken to Anna today. I haven't spoken to her at all.

Harriet I know. I got it all out of Imogen.

Max In between contractions?

Harriet She's not having contractions.

Max But let me guess – you are?

Harriet What are you doing in here?

Max I was just checking the telly.

He picks up a remote control and starts playing with it.

Harriet Where are our guests Max? You organised this party and our guests are staging silent protests in various parts of the house.

Max Doesn't look good, does it?

Harriet This is not a joke.

She turns away from the screen, rearranges some furniture, clears up, etc.

You invite strangers round for drinks. Then you behave like a psychopath all evening.

Max presses a button. On the screen suddenly we see the small girl from earlier up in a tree. She's climbing

*and looking at the camera and laughing, swinging
precariously from the branches. Max looks at the
screen.*

Max Harriet. Harriet –

The little girl is shouting down to another child.

*Unheard dialogue: Anna, 'I'm the king of the castle
and you're the dirty rascal!'*

*She looks at the screen, sees nothing, and then
snatches the remote control off him and puts it away.*

Harriet Just ring the shop up tomorrow and they will
send a five-year-old round to show you how to work it.

Max I'm having a bad day.

Harriet Aren't we all? You don't hold the monopoly on
pain, Max.

He looks at the screen again. The little girl has gone.

I find you increasingly distasteful.

He recovers himself.

Max Why are you suddenly worried about our guests?

Harriet Because – if we can't even do this – if we can't be
together for this, make a show of being together for this,
then what are we doing?

Max But darling, you made solemn vows to me.

Harriet Mmm. 'Till death do us part.' It's got a nice ring
to it, hasn't it?

They look at each other. Marcus enters.

Max Here's one.

Marcus I think I'd like to go home now. But Imogen
wants to stay.

Max There you go, then. The party's a triumph.

Harriet looks at him.

I'll go and round the rest of them up. Imogen! Jacklyn!
Here – kitty, kitty, kitty . . .

He goes out.

Harriet I apologise for my husband, Marcus. Imogen's
looking so well. You must be excited.

Marcus Yes.

Harriet I was always fond of Imogen. I thought she was
a very down-to-earth influence on Anna.

Marcus She's my anchor.

Harriet Oh. Is she?

Marcus Absolutely. She's going to be a wonderful
mother.

Harriet You're very lucky.

Marcus I know.

*Marcus looks at Harriet penetratingly – she bristles
slightly. Pause.*

It was you, wasn't it?

Harriet What?

Marcus It was you I – I – saved today. Outside the
greengrocer's.

Harriet It depends on your perception.

Marcus What?

Harriet How can you save someone who doesn't want to
be saved?

Marcus You walked out on purpose. In front of that car?

Harriet You got in my way.

Marcus No. No. That's not what happened. You're lying. That's not how it happened – I saw the way you looked at me –

He touches her face – she pulls away. She looks away from him.

Harriet I'm sorry to disappoint you.

He looks at her, slightly horrified, as Imogen enters, followed by Jacklyn.

Imogen False alarm! I'm sorry everyone, Mrs Villiers, Harriet. I'm fine. I'm fine. It was a Braxton Hicks.

Jacklyn She's fine.

Imogen Jacklyn's been amazing. Thank God you were here.

Jacklyn I'm here to serve! I didn't do anything really. The doula merely facilitates the mother's journey.

She sits Imogen down, then sits herself.

Marcus I really think we should go home.

Imogen I'm fine, Marcus. The baby's not coming.

Max enters with another bottle of red wine, which he proceeds to open.

Jacklyn Although we've got a hunch that her mucous plug has come out.

Harriet Her what?

Jacklyn Mucous plug.

Imogen My mucous plug.

Max uncorks the bottle of red with a pop.

Max Cheers!

Jacklyn It's a plug of mucus at the entrance to the uterus.

Max Thank God we've cleared that up.

He pours wine for them.

Max (*to Harriet*) You see, darling, the wine's flowing, the mucus is flowing . . .

Harriet Max –

Marcus That's it, I'm taking you home.

Imogen But the mucous plug doesn't mean anything.

Jacklyn It means it could still be a week away. That's just the baby saying, 'Don't forget about me.'

Marcus I really think you'd be better off at home.

Imogen (*firm*) Don't be silly, Marcus. I admit I got a little bit emotional before. But I think we should enjoy ourselves. When are we going to get the chance again? A bit of grown-up conversation.

Max Exactly. A bit of grown-up conversation, I'm sure if we all try really hard we can aspire towards that.

Imogen We haven't even started on Anna yet.

Max Exactly. Come on! It's twenty-one years of colic for you two soon. Have a drink, Marcus. Relax.

He pours him a whisky.

Jacklyn (*who's quite pleased with herself*) She's absolutely fine, Marcus. I'll keep an eye on her. You relax.

Harriet I think you should stay, Marcus. I'd like you to stay.

Max Ah. Harriet has spoken.

Marcus looks at Harriet, then takes his drink. Eddie enters.

Jacklyn Oh, there you are. Where have you been?

Eddie With the children. At the door. I had a little chat with them. Asked them for a trick. That flummoxed them.

Jacklyn laughs.

One little girl appeared to be dressed as Harold Shipman.

Jacklyn No!

Eddie She turned on me a bit when I said I didn't have anything. I couldn't get rid of her.

Max You see, Marcus. This is what you've got in store for you.

Eddie In the end I had to give her a pound to go away.

Jacklyn I've done Reiki on little children – some as little as nine or ten – and you wouldn't believe the emotional blockages.

Harriet You should do some Reiki on Max.

Jacklyn I like to think of it as emotional plumbing. I'm very reasonable. No call-out charge!

Max Ah, but I'm fond of my emotional blockages. They are what make me *me*, after all.

Harriet Max is writing about page-three girls at the moment.

Marcus You're a writer?

Harriet A ghost writer.

Jacklyn What's a ghost writer?

Max Mmm . . . A ghost writer is essentially a disembodied spirit who wanders the world looking for other lives to possess.

Harriet He writes the autobiographies of C-list celebrities.

Jacklyn Do you?

Harriet He's doing Tabby Morris now.

Imogen Who is she exactly?

Harriet Exactly. Who is she?

Max I may never know.

Harriet Oh, but he will enjoy trying to find out.

Max Harriet disapproves. Can you tell?

Harriet I don't care what you write about.

Max As long as I keep you in rugs.

Harriet Exactly.

Jacklyn Who would you like to write about?

Max Sam Cooke. Dead at thirty-three. Nice and short.

Harriet You won't get any dead people, darling. Dead people don't talk. Dead people are hard to write about.

Max To answer your question, Jack, I like writing the autobiographies of silly, glittery celebrities. I like being anonymous. I don't want to stand up and be counted. Christ no!

Harriet Max takes excessive comfort in strangers.

Max Strangers are important, darling. They remind us who our friends really are.

Harriet I agree. I'm closer to some strangers than I am to my own family. Sadly.

Eddie Max makes these celebrities believe in themselves.

Harriet Max, as you can see, has a fan base of one.

Eddie I do think he's good at what he does.

Max Thanks, mate.

Harriet And Max has just rescued his one fan from a life of meaningless dead-end jobs and elevated him to the status of personal assistant.

Max And he's a very fine personal assistant. Very fine.

Jacklyn Do you work, Harriet?

Max laughs.

Harriet (*ignoring him*) I'm a trained pilates teacher.

Max Come on then, darling – let's have a demonstration.

Harriet I'm moving more towards interior design. I recently dressed a house for a friend of mine. Go ahead, Max, take the piss – you know you want to. My husband has no faith in me.

Max Not at all. I think we do the same thing. Harriet tarts up houses. This house principally, but she may well, God willing, branch out to others. And I do the same with people's lives.

Harriet No, you sit all afternoon with your personal assistant watching old films whilst drinking cans of Special Brew.

Marcus Sounds quite good to me.

Imogen Marcus is a civil servant.

Marcus DEFRA.

Jacklyn What-RA?

Marcus The Department for Environment, Food and Rural Affairs.

Max Ah now – there is a job that matters. A job that has ramifications.

Marcus Some of the time. I try to make a difference.

Imogen You get very good benefits.

Marcus None of which involves drinking beer in the afternoon.

Imogen Marcus has a very good package, though.

Jacklyn I think that people are too defined by what they do.

Imogen I just want to be a mother now.

Harriet Do you?

Jacklyn I am so much more than what I do.

Max Your essence is shining through to us, Jack, believe me.

Jacklyn Are you being funny?

Max No, not at all, I'd love to write your autobiography. You'd make a very good subject.

Jacklyn (*pleased*) Really?

Max You seem to have a very strong sense of self.

Jacklyn I've worked at it. You have to work at it. It's so important. To know who you are.

Max I envy you.

Jacklyn Do you?

Max Self-knowledge is the hardest thing.

Jacklyn Who'd want to read about me, though?

She looks at Eddie. Pause

Eddie When I was in the monastery I lost myself. I lost myself completely.

Max You never told me that.

Pause

Eddie I had to strip everything away. That was the point. All the things, all the ways that I defined myself were gone. Friends, family, even what I looked like. I didn't look at myself in a mirror for two years. Not that it's a habit of mine, as you can probably tell, but to forget your own face, you know, it was hard. Like gold being tested in fire, that's what they say. I thought I'd be so good. I'd thought about it for so long. Had it inside me for so long. But I was struggling, you know. So I went to another brother, Brother Bruno, and asked him to help me and he said that I just had to accept. That once you accepted that all the usual standards for a good life were gone, that then I would discover that I still had a life and one that was filled with richness and wonder and beauty. That I had to make way for my deeper identity – my capacity to feel love and experience joy. That my awareness of being part of something larger and more meaningful should not depend upon my physical comfort, the ability to do things in the world, or even the ability to think about things in a particular, familiar way. That the struggling would never stop, you know, but that once I accepted this I would have a burning sense of who I was.

Harriet And did you?

Eddie Fleetingly perhaps. In isolated moments. But mostly I felt like a failure. I couldn't accept. I would try and pray but images of my past life would be floating through my head. People, places I'd been. (*He looks at Harriet.*) I couldn't get rid of them. I couldn't lose myself to find myself again. I wasn't strong enough. I'm not made of gold. So I came out. I remember the first time I looked in the mirror I didn't know myself at all. It was shocking, you know. It scared me.

Max Thank God you came out.

Eddie I suppose I feel like myself when I see myself in relief to other people. I'm weak like that.

Jacklyn That's not weak. I hate being by myself.

Eddie I'm still waiting for my deeper identity to emerge. I've a sneaking feeling I just don't have one.

The others laugh gently.

I heard from him. A while ago. Brother Bruno. He was dying of cancer. And I felt the strangest thing. I felt jealous of him.

Harriet Why?

Eddie Of his courage, you know. Of his ability to struggle. To persevere. To engage himself. I thought, he'll know exactly how to do it. He'll do it so well.

Harriet Yes.

Pause.

Eddie Sorry, I didn't mean to . . .

The doorbell goes. The screen pings into action. We see the ancient yew tree. We circle it, take in its huge girth.

Eddie I'll go. I'm ready for them this time.

Max looks at the tree on the screen.

Max No.

Eddie (*frowning*) Max?

The image starts to fade. The doorbell goes again.

Max (*recovering himself*) Give them penance, brother.
Ten hail Marys and a How's Your Father.

Eddie smiles and goes. Max smiles after him.

Imogen He's sweet, isn't he?

Max We're thinking of making little chocolate figurines
out of him.

Max starts refilling drinks. He refills Imogen's glass.

Imogen How would you write about me then, Max?
Would I be a good subject?

Max You, my darling? You're a cinch to ghost. Younger
of two. Camden School for Girls. Friend of Anna,
loyal and true. Promising hockey player. Made a very
convincing, nay seminal, portrayal of Joseph of
Arimathea in the school play.

Imogen Pontius Pilate. I was Pontius Pilate.

Max And you got him down to a tee, believe me.
Married far too young. For love. But only really came
into her own once she became a mother. Lived happily
ever after.

Imogen Oh, I like this game.

*Eddie re-enters and sits quietly near Jacklyn, who
smiles at him.*

What about Marcus?

Marcus (*irritated*) Imo –

Max Well, now, that's trickier because I don't actually
know the facts. But that will not stop me. I would say
that Mr Cumberbatch is one of three boys.

Imogen He is! You are, Marcus!

Max Middle son. The plodder.

Imogen Ahh! No. Youngest.

Max Grew up in Godalming. Minor public school. Undistinguished academically, although tried hard. Always tried hard. Our Marcus is a study in neutrality. Took a tab of Ecstasy once. Had no effect on him whatsoever. Marcus is good at toeing the line, paying his parking fines promptly. He thinks deeply about farming, fucking and the food chain.

Marcus That's enough –

Max But he has a secret yearning – we all do – to tread the untrodden path. Marcus yearns to leave his conventional space-deprived life and abandon his wife and unborn child and dwell in a stream-filled valley in North Staffs.

Imogen That's not very nice.

Marcus I happen to love my wife.

Harriet Good for you, Marcus.

Imogen We never argue.

Marcus My wife allows me to be myself.

Max I'm filling up.

Marcus You don't know me. You know nothing about me. Who I am. A . . . a person's . . . inner life. The thoughts I have as I'm falling asleep each night. They are my business and nobody else's.

Imogen What thoughts do you have?

Marcus Nobody can know another person absolutely.

Harriet No.

Marcus Even a husband and wife. And that's as it should be. Some things are private.

Imogen What thoughts, Marcus? You're worrying me now.

Marcus Don't be silly, Imogen. You're missing the point.

Harriet I'm sorry, Marcus. Max has a nasty streak. He can't help himself. He is also a coward.

Max What?

Harriet You're a coward, darling.

The doorbell goes. Eddie gets up to go. Suddenly the screen pings into life again. We see the young girl come out of the tree. She is crying and in a panic. She runs away from the tree, through the wood.

Max reacts. He is breathing heavily. Eddie stops to watch him.

Eddie Max?

Max (*quietly, looking at the screen*) I am. I'm a coward. Forgive me, Marcus.

Harriet What's wrong with you tonight?

He looks at the screen, at the young girl who is running frantically through the wood. The image starts to fade.

Eddie Max?

The image has gone. Max starts to recover.

Max My daughter is far braver than me . . . I shy away from the front line . . . If I was in a full suit of armour, and Sam Cooke and the London Community Gospel Choir were at my arm, singing Amen to my every word, I would still lack courage. If sweet Jesus himself were here, asking me to down tools and join his so solid crew, I would still lack conviction.

Jacklyn I've had experience of the front line.

Eddie Have you?

Jacklyn I'm a member of the Sealed Knot.

Max The what?

Jacklyn It's a historical re-enactment society. We do the English Civil War.

Max (*recovered now*) Oh, wacky Jackie, I bloody love you. You save the day, you do! What would we do without you this evening!

She laughs.

Jacklyn Oh yes, I'm a Knotter, all right!

Max Now, let's get the facts straight, are you a Roundhead or a Cavalier?

Jacklyn I'm a Cavalier, but if numbers are short I don't mind being a Roundhead. I'm in Sir Marmaduke Rawdon's Regiment of Foote. My ex-boyfriend, Gonk, was a unit commander.

Imogen His name is Gonk? That's unusual.

Marcus Before you start getting any ideas, we're not calling the baby Gonk, Imogen.

Harriet Gonk Cumberbatch.

Marcus She's come up with worse, believe me.

Jacklyn It's not his real name. He won't tell anyone what his real name is. We met at the Battle of Cropredy Bridge. He was a bit mad, though. We went out for a year. But the battles got him very worked up – he always went too far in the beer tent afterwards. We split up six months ago at the Siege of Gloucester. I want to change regiment now.

Imogen So do the women get to fight too?

Jacklyn I'm mostly a civilian, but because I'm a trained first-aider I get to be a medic and see the action up close. Last muster I went to I got to fire a cannon. They've said I can train as a pikeman. It's funny, I'm a very non-combative sort of person in real life but there's something about charging with a sixteen-foot iron pike that really appeals.

Max What about Eddie? How do you think he'll shape up? Could he be a musketeer, do you think?

Jacklyn If he wants to. I see him more as a drummer.

Max Little drummer boy, yes!

Jacklyn The drummers were very educated. They were sent to parley with the enemy. (*To Eddie, smiling.*) The Battle of Bosworth is coming up, if you're interested.

Max Now there's a venue for a date.

Jacklyn Can't be worse than this one.

Pause.

Imogen (*brightly*) Marcus was very brave this morning.

Marcus No I wasn't –

Imogen Yes you were, with that woman. Tell them.

Marcus No.

Imogen He saved a woman's life.

Marcus I didn't.

Imogen Yes you did.

Marcus Imo –

Imogen What?

Marcus I don't want to –

Imogen Oh, don't be silly – you were a hero!

Marcus Imogen! Just leave it, okay?

Harriet No, come on, Marcus. Tell us. Why not?

Max Have we got a have-a-go hero in our midst?

Imogen Yes we have!

Max Call the *Ham and High* immediately! Are we talking front page?

Imogen No, I'm being serious –

Max So am I! Oh, spill the beans, your heroism will not go unsung here.

Marcus It was nothing. A woman stepped out in front of a car. I held her back, that's all.

Imogen You wrestled her onto a car boot!

Max Good God!

Jacklyn How old was she?

Marcus I didn't get a good look at her.

Jacklyn What did she say?

Marcus Nothing.

Imogen She didn't thank him.

Jacklyn It must have been the shock.

Max Women often have a very cavalier attitude towards the Green Cross Code.

Imogen She looked straight through him – just waltzed into the greengrocer's.

Max Typical. When you look deeply into a woman's eyes, there's almost always a mental shopping list going on.

Marcus I think she was relieved. The way she looked at me.

Harriet How did she look at you?

Marcus Almost like she loved me.

Imogen You didn't tell me that.

Harriet Like she loved you?

Marcus Yes.

Harriet I think you're exaggerating.

Marcus No.

Harriet Why would she love you?

Marcus Because she wanted to live.

Pause.

Harriet You must feel quite the hero.

Marcus (*rattled*) Perhaps she didn't want me to save her. But in a way that doesn't concern me – I would do the same thing again. If I were to see someone, anyone – even a complete stranger – in danger or in pain, I would try to help them. I wouldn't be able to stop myself.

Max May you be instantly decorated. A medal for conspicuous bravery!

Eddie I'm sure she felt grateful later – after you'd gone – when it was too late to thank you.

Harriet Either that or she'll prosecute you for assault.

The doorbell goes. The screen pings into life. We see the ancient yew tree. Max looks at it. The camera is circling it once more.

Marcus I'll go!

Harriet No, no, you sit down. You've done enough for one day.

Marcus I'd like to . . . get some air.

He exits towards the door. Max looks away from the screen. He starts to refill drinks again.

Imogen (*calling after him*) Marcus! He's upset. You've upset him.

Max He's fine. Marcus can take care of himself. He's a national treasure. He should be publicly installed at Beachy Head.

Imogen Marcus is brave. He's very brave. You don't know anything.

Max It's just a joke, Imo. Don't get your knickers in a twist.

Imogen It's not a joke. I know you look down on me. Me and Mr Cumberbatch. God, you'll laugh about us afterwards, won't you, in your beautiful superking bed with Egyptian cotton sheets.

Max Don't be silly, darling-

Imogen I'm not your darling.

Max (*pouring drinks*) I'm in awe of Marcus. You wouldn't think he had it in him, would you, to look at him? Scrawny little thing. But no. Make sure you don't have a death wish round Marcus. He'll beat the living shit out of you.

Imogen Your daughter's the one with the death wish.

Max Anna is putting her life at risk, for others. I would agree with you there.

Imogen No. She was always having sex with strangers. In parks, you know. Casual sex. From when she was twelve or thirteen.

Suddenly we see the young girl on the screen. She is standing in front of the tree. On the far side of the tree

*is an old, overgrown graveyard. She stands perfectly
still, looking at or almost beyond the camera. Her face
is strangely impassive*

Max What are you talking about?

Imogen She was off her face on stuff, of course, but she
said it was the only thing that made her feel alive. Anna
sleeps with anyone she wants to. I'm sure she's not fussy
even now – Palestinians, Israelis, she'll be like, bring it
on. Doing her own little international peace effort.

Max This is deeply hurtful –

Imogen I was her friend, her best friend, I loved her, we
did everything together and she just discarded me. I wasn't
good enough for her. She made me look like a bloody
fool.

Max Why are you saying all this?

Imogen I'm saying it because it's true. I'm saying it
because we all have a right to be heard, don't we?
However dull and ugly and useless we are, isn't that
right, Eddie?

Eddie I don't know.

Harriet You should be out there. In Israel. Not Anna.

Max Harriet –

Harriet Well, look at her – she'd give a bulldozer a
bloody good run for its money.

Imogen If I had the choice of standing in front of a tank
or living with you two, I know which I'd rather.

Jacklyn Stop this. It doesn't matter, Imogen – it doesn't
matter about the past –

Imogen It does matter!

Jacklyn But you're so lucky! You're so young and you're with Marcus and you're having a baby!

Imogen You don't know anything about me. I'm not lucky. Oh, I know he's attractive – people tell me I've done very well for myself. But I find it so hard to look at him when he comes.

Pause.

Marcus re-enters. During the following the image of Anna remains on the screen. Max looks at it.

Marcus It's a beautiful night. Chilly but bright. What? What have I missed?

Jacklyn I feel the need to do some urgent Reiki on you, Marcus.

Marcus I'm fine, really. Had a stroll round the block. Feel much better for some air.

Imogen I want a drink. Wet the baby's head.

Marcus Shall I make you some tea?

Imogen No, fuck that, wine, please. Relax me.

He takes her glass, refills it.

Imogen I was just saying how Max thought all Anna's friends fancied him. When we were at school. But I never did.

Jacklyn Eddie. I want to go.

Marcus What's going on?

Jacklyn This is not a good place for me right now. I'm very delicate. I take on other people's pain.

Imogen I was telling them how my parents divorced when I was twelve and what a relief it was to all concerned.

That if they'd carried on they might have ended up like Max and Harriet. Perish the thought!

Marcus Imo! This isn't like you!

Imogen Isn't it? It feels quite like me.

Harriet (*talking to Max, about Imogen*) I want her out of my house, Max.

Imogen Really? You're like a second daughter to us, that's what you used to say to me.

Jacklyn Eddie. Why did you bring me here?

Eddie I'm sorry – it was a mistake –

Jacklyn Do you dislike me?

Eddie No, no, not at all. I don't know you-

Jacklyn Oh I get it! I know what this is all about! Had your little joke have you, at my expense?

Eddie What?

Jacklyn You and your posh mates. That's why you brought me here, is it? To humiliate me.

Eddie I thought this would be better – less pressurised –

Jacklyn Less pressurised! You don't understand. I'm thirty-nine and I'm pre-menopausal. I don't have time for all this.

Eddie I was wrong. I shouldn't have-

Jacklyn DO YOU HEAR ME – I AM RUNNING OUT OF TIME!

Eddie I hear you.

Jacklyn (*quietly, starting to cry*) I thought I sensed substance from you. Real substance. Thought you were the quiet, thoughtful type. Thought you wouldn't fuck me over, like the others. But you know what, I think I was wrong. I think what I thought was substance was absence.

Eddie You might be right there.

Jacklyn Do you know how hard it was for me to talk to you today?

Eddie I 'm sorry – I couldn't think where else to take you.

Jacklyn That's pathetic.

Eddie It is – it is, I know. I'll make it up to you.

Jacklyn I can't go home on my own any more. Please. Don't make me. I'm so lonely. I have no life. I have absolutely no life.

Eddie You do. I'm sorry. Don't cry. It's all my fault.

Jacklyn I'm trying so hard. I'm doing my best. I always do my best.

Harriet I know how you feel.

Marcus Imogen? What's been happening? I insist you tell me.

Imogen We've been doing our own little Halloween thing. Letting off steam.

Suddenly Max moves towards Imogen.

Max (erupting, to imogen) That's it! That is it! You have said enough! You be quiet now!

The image of Anna on the screen fades.

Marcus Please don't talk like that to my wife. She's nine months' pregnant.

Max Well, why don't you take the poor defenceless thing home?

Marcus Now look here –

Max We are cumbered by you, Cumberbatch. We find you and your wife a big fucking cumbrance. Please, I beg you, encumber us no longer.

Marcus You two are seriously fucked up.

Max Are we? Well, let me tell you, mate, right now I'd rather be in my shoes. After what she's told us. Oh yes.

Marcus Really?

Imogen Don't listen to them, Marcus.

Marcus You think my marriage is in a worse state than yours?

Max I'd take bets on it.

Marcus Really? Well at least my wife didn't try to top herself this morning.

Max What?

Marcus The woman who stepped out in front of the car, the woman who was ready to embrace death, was none other than your beautiful, fragrant wife.

Max What?

Marcus You want to look to your own, Villiers.

Max Harriet?

Marcus There are troubled spots closer to home than you might think.

Imogen (*with some relish*) Oh dear.

Max Harriet?

Harriet I told you I'd had a stressful day.

> *Pause.*

Max Did you buy the rug before or after?

Harriet What?

Max Before or after you tried to walk in front of the car?

Harriet Before. What are you getting at?

Max She didn't want to die, then.

Harriet What?

Max You don't know my wife. She would never kill herself when there is a PIN number still to give out.

Harriet You think you're so clever, don't you?

Max You bought the rug – you were thinking about the rug – 'Is it too red? Too green? Will it go with the wood in our front room?' You were distracted – if a fucking double-decker bus had been coming at you, you wouldn't have seen it.

Harriet That's right – you talk it all away.

Max I'm right, though, aren't I? You might like the drama of the other version, but in fact you were just a tad careless. Crisis over. We've cleared that one up, so the Cumberbatches can leave now.

Harriet That's it. Sweep it all under – the – (*She stops herself.*)

Max The new carpet? Unfortunate use of metaphor, darling, but surprisingly apposite too.

Harriet Do you want to hear what happened today? I'll tell you what happened today.

Max No need. I can see it all. Rug. Worried about rug. Oh dear, nearly died. Walked into greengrocer's. Hah! Now is that the action of a suicidal woman, I ask you? You were already on to the next thing – thinking what a lovely dinner you'd rustle up for your hardworking husband –

Harriet I fucked my rug man! I had sex with the man who sold me the rug. Burak – my rug man. My lovely young brown-skinned rug man. I fucked him on the fucking rug.

Pause.

Marcus (*to Max*) I'd take the rug back if I was you.

Max What do you want me to say?

Harriet I had sex with him and it was good, I felt released.

Imogen Like mother, like daughter.

Max You felt so good you ran in front of a car?

Harriet I don't know why you're so bothered – you were salivating over Tabby Morris at the same time.

Max Tabby Morris doesn't want me.

Harriet What?

Max She doesn't want me.

Harriet Oh God! The rejection! You're past it, Max! It's official! How will you cope?

Max She doesn't want me as a writer.

Harriet Got a bit too flirty, did you? I have a new-found respect for that girl.

Max I have never been unfaithful to you.

Harriet That's not true.

Max It is true.

Harriet Every room we've ever walked into with a Tabby Morris in it, it's passed through your head –

Max No –

Harriet You forget I'm even there.

Max That's not true.

Harriet You may not sleep with them, but you think about it –

Max I have never been unfaithful to you.

Harriet In your head you have – a thousand times, you have – and that is as bad. I feel like nothing. I fucked my rug man and I still feel like nothing because the only man I've ever loved doesn't look at me any more.

Max You're talking bollocks – you're guilty –

Eddie Stop it, both of you –

Jacklyn I think the pair of you are under a lot of stress –

Max We don't need the New Age bollocks now, thank you. Jack and her fucking lantern. That's the last thing we need.

Jacklyn Oh, I know it's easy to take the piss out of me. Because I believe in lots of things and you believe in nothing.

Max Well – maybe that makes me happy. Maybe believing in nothing floats my fucking boat.

Jacklyn You're not happy. Not even close. You're worried about your daughter, it's understandable – she's your only child –

Max She's not our only child.

Harriet Yes she is.

Max No.

Harriet Max. Don't you fucking dare.

Max I have denied his existence once today, I will not do it again.

Harriet This is me. Please don't talk about him.

Eddie Some things should be talked about.

Harriet (*turning on him viciously*) You fuck off, Eddie Fox. You are not a member of this family – you do not belong here – you have no right –

Max We have a son. Freddie. Freddie. I will bear witness to him, Harriet, I will. He deserves that. His name is Freddie. And he is dead. He is dead. He died when he was seven years old.

Harriet Please don't. Max, I beg you.

During the next Harriet starts to cry silently.

Max Harriet and I cannot talk about him. And yet we are defined by his absence.

Jacklyn Oh God.

Max He died fifteen years ago.

Harriet Please don't.

Marcus (*to Imogen*) Did you know about this?

Imogen It was before I met Anna. I knew, but she never talked about him.

Max Nobody talks about him.

Pause.

Eddie Freddie had dark, curly hair and brown eyes. He was a very beautiful child, full of mischief. He was obsessed with magic, with spells. He was funny and clever and everything a child should be.

Marcus How did he die?

Eddie He was struck by lightning. It was a tragic accident. They were on a camping holiday. Anna and Freddie went to play in the woods when a storm came on very suddenly. The rain was very heavy and they sheltered under a tree.

Max An ancient yew tree.

Eddie He was hit by a side flash and died instantly.

Max Anna couldn't do anything.

Eddie Anna was ten years old and she tried to shield him but she could not.

> *The screen pings into life. We see the story of Anna and Freddie as we have seen it played out on the screen this evening but in very short, spiky jump cuts. This time our focus of attention is the little boy who was always just out of sight. We see Anna and Freddie running laughing through the woods. Freddie picking up a stick and chasing her round the tree. Anna climbing the tree and little Freddie watching her. Anna taking Freddie's hand. Then we jump to the yew tree. Jump cut to Anna stepping inside, followed by Freddie. Jump cut to the two children inside the tree. Jump cut to Anna putting her arm around Freddie. The two children looking upwards. Anna running outside distraught. Anna standing impassively. The dialogue continues through the film.*

Marcus That's very sad.

Jacklyn Poor Anna.

> *On the screen we move round the tree away from Anna. We stand in front of it and look at it as if we were looking from Max's point of view. The image is now almost static – but the leaves should sway slightly in the wind. Perhaps we hear the sounds of a wood, ever so faintly: some birdsong, wind. The dialogue is continuous.*

Max I used to go to the tree. Every now and again. By myself. It must be nearly two thousand years old. The tree. Although it's difficult to know with yews. It's old beyond guessing. The trunk is nearly thirty feet in circumference . . . and the middle is almost entirely hollow. You can step inside it – and you're completely covered by the overhead branches. Like a house. If I had been looking for a tree to shelter in I would have chosen this one. The trunk is fantastically knotted . . . in places the bark has been stripped away and you can see the heartwood underneath. It's a beautiful tree, a wise tree, but it failed to save my son.

Pause.

And every night when I close my eyes I see the lightning play with his body.

The doorbell goes.

Harriet (*quietly, distraught*) Freddie is mine. How dare you. Parade him in front of strangers. He is mine. He is my darling. You know that. You can have Anna. Anna doesn't love me.

Max Of course she does.

Harriet She's always been yours. But Freddie is mine.

Max He is mine too.

Harriet You found him! You just found him.

Max Anna led me to him.

Harriet You found him and he was dead.

Max I couldn't save him. He was already dead.

Harriet And you carried on living. How could you do that?

Max In the same way that you did.

She is sobbing now.

Harriet No. We are not the same.

Max I went on living for you. And for Anna. Because that was all that was left for me to do.

Harriet But I don't want to live. I don't want to live any more. I've tried. All this time I've tried. I don't want it any more.

Eddie looks at Max.

Eddie Max?

Max does not move. Eddie goes to her. Eddie kneels beside her.

Harriet –

She looks directly at Eddie.

Harriet I was tired of feeling numb. I wanted to feel real pain. And then for it to be over.

Eddie I know.

He holds her. She resists him.

Harriet No, I don't want this.

Eddie I know you don't.

Harriet I want you to go.

Eddie I can't leave you. I've tried. But I can't.

Harriet Please. My little boy. I just want my little boy. That's all I want. That's not much to ask, is it?

Eddie No.

Harriet Please help me. Eddie.

Eddie This is why I'm here. Harriet. This is why I'm always here.

She gives herself up to him. He holds her. She cries.

Harriet Oh God. Please help me. Please please help me.

Her crying starts to subside as Eddie comforts her.

Eddie (*quietly*) Shhh. Shhh.

Silence. Max is suffering greatly. The doorbell goes again. The image of the tree starts to dissolve. Imogen goes to go.

Max Nobody move.

She stands to go again.

I said sit down.

Imogen But they're just children.

Max Yes. But they are the wrong children. They are always the wrong children.

They sit in silence. On the screen the image changes from the tree. Slowly flickering into life we see the children at the door. A small group of children of various shapes and sizes all dressed in Halloween costumes. They look expectantly at the door. They ring again. We hear the doorbell. Harriet slowly stops crying. It is as though the children outside and the adults inside are listening to one another. Suddenly Imogen gets up again.

Imogen Oh my God. Something's happening.

Marcus What is it, Imo?

Imogen The baby.

She staggers towards the rug. She raises her hands in the air and groans – a strange primeval sound. At the same time we have strobe lighting – like lightning. All the characters move – trying to help her or moving back to give her room. She stands with her legs akimbo and her waters break. On the screen we see flickering images of all the children we have seen throughout the play running wildly in all different directions through the woods. We hear the noise of children – talking, laughing, singing – a jumbled soundtrack of childhood. The children all run away. Suddenly the lights come back on. There is silence and the images on the screen disappear.

Jacklyn Her waters have broken.

Imogen starts to contract.

Marcus Are you in pain?

Imogen is winded by her first contraction.

Imo?

Imogen This is it. This is it.

Jacklyn She's having a contraction.

Marcus Breathe, Imo. That's it. Good girl.

Jacklyn Slowly.

Marcus Are you okay? Imo?

She speaks with difficulty through the contraction.

Imogen I said terrible things. I don't know why I said them.

Marcus It doesn't matter.

Imogen I will tell you what I said.

Marcus I don't need to know.

She gives herself up to the contraction.

Imogen It's stopping, it's going. It was quite intense though.

Jacklyn Good girl.

Imogen I love you, Marcus.

Marcus I love you too.

Jacklyn We need to get you to hospital. I think there was some meconium in your waters.

Imogen Is the baby in distress? Marcus – the baby's in distress!

Jacklyn We'll just get you checked out.

Marcus I'll ring ahead. I'll go and bring the car round.

He dithers, panicky.

Max (*kindly, to him*) Do you want me to get it? The car?

Marcus No. No. I can go.

Marcus exits.

Imogen (*to Jacklyn*) Will you come with me?

Jacklyn Of course I will.

Eddie Jacklyn –?

Imogen Oh no. I think another one's coming.

Jacklyn I'll time it this time.

Jacklyn looks at her watch, times the contraction.

Imogen Agh!

Max Here, hold my hand. Grip as hard as you can.

She grasps his hand.

Eddie Jacklyn?

Max That's it. Break my fingers. I don't need to write any more. It's all fucking rubbish anyway.

Eddie Jacklyn. Time is running out for me, too.

Pause.

It's been running out for the last thirty years.

Jacklyn (*to Imogen, but looking at Eddie*) That's right, Imogen.

The contraction subsides.

Imogen It's finished. That one's finished.

Eddie Soon I'll have nothing to show for it. Nothing at all.

Jacklyn That one was forty-five seconds.

Imogen I didn't think it'd be like this. It really hurts.

She looks at Eddie.

Jacklyn Yes, it does.

She looks back at Imogen.

Jacklyn Don't worry, this baby's going to be out in no time.

Max Can you walk?

Imogen Yes.

Harriet Her shoes. Don't forget your shoes.

Max takes the shoes from Harriet.

Imogen (*looks at Harriet*) I'm scared.

Harriet (*touching her*) Don't be. You're on your way now.

Imogen I want to meet him. The baby.

Harriet Of course you do.

Imogen (*to Eddie*) Say a prayer for me.

Jacklyn exits with Imogen. Max exits too, supporting her. Eddie and Harriet stand apart. Silence. The storm passes. They look at the rug. The laughter grows in them during the next.

Eddie Harriet.

Harriet What?

Eddie I hate to tell you this.

Harriet What?

Eddie The rug.

Harriet I know.

Eddie It's ruined.

Harriet I know.

Eddie You won't be able to take it back.

Harriet Amniotic fluid. And meconium.

Eddie What is that?

Harriet Shit, I think. It's shit.

Eddie It is shit.

They both start to laugh. They laugh. They stop. Pause. A sad pause.

You and Max.

Harriet Yes.

Eddie You have been storm-chasing for a long time.

Harriet Yes.

Pause.

I wish he felt about me the way he feels about you.

Eddie He loves you. Immensely.

Harriet I know.

She looks at Eddie. Max re-enters.

How was Imogen?

Max In pain. They're coming thick and fast.

Harriet It's funny to think of a completely new person being born tonight.

Eddie (*looking at his watch*) Tomorrow now. All Saints' Day.

She goes to go.

Max Harriet?

Harriet I'm going to see my daughter now. Wherever she is. She's been on her own for too long. She is mine too. I carried her. She is mine.

Max Of course she is.

Harriet Someone needs to shield her.

Max Let me come with you.

Harriet No. Please.

Pause.

I'm sorry.

Max Yes.

Harriet I'm so sorry.

Max So am I.

Harriet There's nothing more to say, is there?

Max There's always more to say.

Harriet No, Max.

Max This is not a full stop. This is a comma. Or a semi-colon – you can give me that.

Harriet I don't know.

Max But what will I do? On my own?

Harriet You'll have to be brave. Don't worry, Eddie's here.

Max looks at Eddie.

Eddie We can drink beer. Play our music loud.

She turns and exits. Pause.

Max There was a time after Freddie died when you used to come and sit up with me, all night, without saying anything.

Eddie Where else was I going to go?

Pause.

Max Get the beers in, then.

Eddie goes and gets beers. While he is gone, Max tries the TV. It switches on immediately and normally, in colour. We see a contemporary news item.

It's working! The telly's working.

He looks at it. It does not satisfy him. He switches it off. He switches the stereo on. It is Sam Cooke singing 'This Little Light of Mine'. Eddie re-enters.

Eddie (*at the choice of music*) Agh!

They open cans of beer. They sit down.

Max Do you think you'll see Jack again?

Eddie Hope so. Doubt it.

A rumble of thunder interrupts the song. They stare ahead.

Max I'm not brave, Eddie.

Eddie Neither am I.

The song is distorted by the thunder in the distance.
They stare ahead.

It'll be all right.

Suddenly Max gets up and lights the pumpkin face.
He brings it down and places it on the floor between
them.

Max Strength in numbers.

Eddie nods his agreement. The stage reverts to
woodland. The rain pours. They sit. They face the
storm.

Eddie We'll outstare the lightning.

Sam Cooke sings.

Sam Cooke: 'Amen. Amen. Amen. Amen. I wonder
would everyone join me on the last chorus? Everybody?
Amen. Amen. A little louder? Amen. With the spirit?
Amen. Amen. Amen.'

There is lightning flash after lightning flash. They stare
ahead.

Blackout.

The End.